THOSE GRIEVING RAINDROPS

ROB VOGEL

Ordering Information:

Prime Seven Media
518 Landmann St.
Tomah City, WI 54660

Printed in the United States of America

This is a book of poetry, imagery and prose created by Rob Vogel

I wanted to further express my feelings
and visually illustrate them.
It doesn't matter how it is written, as
long as something is said.
On the floor, I am more at ease. I feel nearer,
more part of my actual writing,
since this way I can walk around it, work from the
four sides and literally be part of the story.
When I'm writing, I'm not aware of what I'm doing;

It's only after an acquainted time period
that I read what I've been writing.
I've no fears about making changes to
my text as it has a life of its own,
I don't write about things; I write only about
the differences between things...
Poetry is an emotion, a product and ideas.
It is what I dream of, and a balance of
true purity, fantasy and serenity;

That include trouble or depressing subject matters a
soothing, calming influence on the mind,
rather like a good armchair which provides
relaxation from physical fatigue;

The text is created in English, as I lived for
many years in the Republic of Ireland,

A country of myth's, creativity, art, music and fantasy.
I have been writing and painting for many years,
as savage creator and satirist, my approach
is to stand back and let our mind create the
full story and give it the freedom
to make its own decisions.
His intense reluctance and hate for fame, is
well known by his family and friends.
As his original language was not English
but Dutch, he loved to use
the English language as it is more creative and
has a different way of explaining feelings and
failures, in each writing ventures, all
must have a beginning and an end.

Undisciplined emotions must be conquered
and put in their correct place,

This bundle is a group of prose, sonnets and rhyming prose,
with no guidelines towards love, guild or living, it is only
a small bundle of a much larger selection of my poetry.

---

*"At age of us, thine eagle's goes on its soaring
flight, and sweeps beyond our view"*

TABLE OF CONTENTS

PASSED

I just passed you, some time ago, my dear,
It was that August night filled with that ripening
moon, alive and sharp, you were, full of cheer,
You came to me in the midst the night, so soon;

With quietude, and sultriness, you did slumber,
And at your mouth a new refrain showed, so sweet,
Harmony, in that warm night of summer,
While that silken veil of light fell at your feet;

And the full-orbed moon, soared into my soul,
I have to say goodbye, to those sweet rays,
The pearly luster of that moon lit sole,
Roses grew in an enchanted way those days;

Was it not fate that, when on that August close,
I breathed the incense of that still slumbering rose?

WONDERING

Let me not admit the merging of minds,
I will survive my well-contended day,
Compare them with the bettering of when blind,
Reserved for my rhyme, to keeps love at bay;

When out to in the woods, my muse does grow,
I admit them impediments, it's not love,
That looks on tempests and 'twill never show,
Love alters not with brief hours I behoove;

Is it the stars in every wandering tree?
Through hollow groves and the hilly lands.
I walk and dream of flames shunned by those bees,
Within his bending sickle I come to stand;

And walk till work and times are done and clean,
Before I will find out where she has been.

BULLFIGHT

Do not be gentle in this day of rage,
Facing the anguish on his sandy stage,
Today is his war, with color 'nd dead,
Taunted, in agony, color, and noise, he bled;

Thought unequivocally he had the upper hand,
But that single shaft burst in, not as plann'd,
A matador, the best with his red cape,
Issues the last orders to finish in fluid shape;

Rage, against the bulls, dying in the light,
Two souls that have not grown up, in spite,
Of my heart that has taken a stand against,
His frail deeds, his light dance barely sensed;

Do not be gentle in this day of rage,
And fight, against the bull, dying of the light.

ETERNITY

As I stand beneath that mystic moon,
Dewy and dim with its golden rim,
Flowers ripe and softly nodding at my sight,
Eternity does not rest, nor does I know where it goes;

As ruin's molder, I sleep in peace,
While wizards rout and move the cloud's roof,
Ships leave their mooring, deserting their posts,
I envy the seas upon where they always ride;

On those speechless flowing saline hills,
Dreams are created that end into the watery graves;
Without those hapless ships, men all 're doomed,
As they cannot dwell on this shore;

I pray and wait, as that she may be there,
With my unopened eyes will I see,
While the dim sheeted ghosts goes by,
Let the moon hide in this everlasting night;

As a reverie came over m' hoping,
Would I exchange you, for my fields and forests?
My ancient name, my ruins and heart,
My ancestors, with whom I soon shall lie?

DREAMS

Will it matter if I'm alive or death,
In spring, when water caress's its shore gently,
That stream from that endless well, it forever drawn's,
And the endless moon hidden in that darkness of the sky;

She looked at me with that haughty look,
As I once vowed to live without mistress,
My bitter heart filled, not feeling pain,
Revived and blossoming like flowers in spring;

As the wan wintery colors fade away,
I see my dreams go by, on by one,
When climbing moon follows those empty ships,
Ships doomed and becalmed on that once wild sea;

A cold wet saline wind blows my dreams away,
I sleep, and I w'll not see those promised dreams.

SPRING

Early morn' I ramble in those spring's fields,
The sweet's air of coming summer 's here anew,
My sense spelled it promise of nature's yields,
As I feasted on day's tremendous dew;

O' why? I wait for winds gusts to becalm,
Against that barren rage as it's cold 'll decay,
Waiting, for that woman in nature's palm,
I am forced to follows season's play?

I draw those tender lines with 'n antique pen,
Seeing woman's heart, but not yet acquainted,
While wandering aimlessly in that flagrant glen,
Following those lines I have so often painted;

O' for that draught of vintage, so good it once was.

NATURE

Spring at noontide 'tis cold 'nd somber,
I looked up at nights mid-time, the moon is like umber,
 Stars shown pale in that darkness,
 That moon 'mid her slaves so weak, but there regardless;
Salty air of the wild place, 's too cold for me,
Covered by a misty shroud but not be hiding the sea,
 In the distance and coming near,
 Is that summer's Sun warm and so dear;
Those Sun's beams, golden and full of fire,
That glory from afar, a light that we all desire,
 I envy those silent hills bathed in that golden light,
 Forbidden when moon 's out during that dark night;
But let me not mar my nightly dreams,
Where I can silence those awful streams,
 I wait during springtime's pallid days,
 Time, when gentians frill in many a way;

Nature is a place for light and morning dew,
So, go your way, and promise ne'er to view,
 That barren cave where I am presumed to hide,
 I couldn't find any privacy where Summer does reside.

A WHISPER

My mind whispers to itself,
And all those past lovers;

But none of them loved me,
As I am buried alive;

According to my expectations,
She is a rose, fighting to bloom.

LADY

She was a Grecian lady, yes, heading home with her gifts,
Fruit and sweet wine, still young she was,

Aboard that fragile ship, holding its own in a foamy sea,
Dawn appeared like a golden tread out of that sweet sky;

Passing those rocks black and foreboding, washed by a foamy
watery spray,
She was brushed from cheek and throat in that hoary way,

Old and ancient during that morn, I looked with longing eyes,
For that passion, mocking her sweet virginity;

But as a mermaid combed her dank and dripping hair,
The stealthy hunter sees th' young lady, and 'll drawn her blood;

As on this beach in that a rocky cave during that day,
There hung the yellow-belled laburnum, standing firm of her;

> Smooth as is the beach, save where some ebbing tides
> once were,
> I we'll soon to forget those garlands on the galley's
> painted prow.

MUSE

Not from heaven's stars do I get knowledge,
Nor do I have the fortune of solace;

But glancing at her fair face,
Adorned with flowing grace;

O' what painter shall we find,
To use those subtle hues and form in mind;

Fleeing swift 'n white-feathered snowy sheet,
Unknown to falsehood or deceit;

But as I read m' rhymes of pale melancholy,
While the sun's radiant bowl 's filled the sky with her folly;

For now, I'll bid these words farewell,
To follow my duty and return to where I do dwell;

THE DARE

Beside that meandering river rill, that's flowing fast,
    New-born sun dried that morn's dew still on its swards,
While sky and that dying mill are old and past,
    We've those wings of wind that blew helping to guard;

As satins flutter in the air as dawns rise,
    Beneath the cloud topped hills I reached out,
A gentle dream we did share without lies,
    And rest beneath gnarled boughs still firm and stout;

Watched for that cloud and gentle winds at dawn,
    In confusing and disorder, we cry our despair,
Am I 'n exquisite trifler or deceiver gone?
    Little tied by vows and promises that are there;

And as this is a shocking liberty of me,
    A frigid glance, the price for daring we agree.

THE VALE

In the cold bare park's shadows pass as blights,
Lips colorless, souls deprived of glow, in spite,
Ghosts of buried pasts, that couldn't last the night, S
hades relent, 'tis was time for their delight;

The dark designs I loved, relinquished since,
And all the evil dreams I had, left, they are,
As souls walk 'mid frozen waste I can't convince,
Of love immortal that's not true so far;

My vision lingers onto that what beautifies them,
Now I live with dark nights and unprinted books,
As their shadows pass springtime not knowing them,
How sweet was hope, during my time it took;

    Our ecstasy past, as it was unwritten,
    Blessed, in those humble vales where our lips met.

AUTUMN'S COMING

Hear that gentle sleep that once was so good,
That darksome sleep gives its yearning to all,
It's discreet, light, and feminine it would,
A whiff of wind o'er buds in early Fall.

And when those sweeping gusts of Autumn blow,
Devoid of kindness and goodness of life,
My heart thinks of glorious summer's glow,
And not that of envy, hatred, and strife.

A blue-sky smiles above that tender roof,
Will it rule the empire in its decline?
Like composing acrostics without any proof,
Moonlight bright as beauty and love sublime.

     We are alone, and pensively as we strolled,
     While ancient aspen rustle' and Autumn rolls in.

FOOLS DREAM

When you're old and sit by candlelight,
By that crackling fire, noisy, but still,
You will recite the verses, I still write,
And sing them in the clear night, without skill,

Alas, as I see my village, green and ripe,
With that chimney smoking in that season of the year,
While on that summer's eve I'll walk along paths I type,
Trampling that once fine grass, with no fear,

But this infinite love will rise and fill my soul,
When I'm away, a bohemian, vivacious, a shadow's bliss,
She might tell me, of her history, that I stole,
Her eyes batting that I will softly kiss,

> Then I feel the wind teasing me, as soft hair gleam,
> A floating white lily, in the thought of a foolish dream.

SUMMER AWAKING

My memory of fantasy, deep beyond the sanguine idea's in
my mind,
A universe of stars, whirls and mirrored flowing rivers,
While the fullness of the moon, illuminate my garden of
nocturnal beauty,
My sentry will endure the ensuing of the dawn, promised to me.

I am myself, like the warped water wheel turning in those
quiet times,
Waiting for that promised summer replacing the fading spring,
The once dark forest, now alive and snaring life,
I watch this countryside awaken, to its emerald and golden day.

Alas, nights confer with day in sulphureous dreams,
An incomprehensible dream, and sleep that never came,
In which withered branches weave their tortured shapes,
Wrought during those dark winter's nights, create anguish
inside me.

Yet, they're slaves of darkness, once profound in winters days,
But I see the walls of paradise, as the sun appears,
Beauty is what surrounds me, flesh and spirit to be admired
with tender gaze,
Summer's warmth and laughter flows, to be acquired.

But blunted by memory and mystery, that aura of power flows,
Unbeknown to me, of those lips, like a hummingbird I will drink,
The planet gave live to us my dear summer,
I will witness you, a hurricane of life, and the thrill of fulfilment.

DARK NIGHTS

There is no need for words now, when I descend into the world
beyond,
A world of dreams, lies and the sinuous illusions of life; that
I can't abscond.
Carried on wings of burn'd glass, I try to extent my horizon
of dreams,
As I look in that mirror, trying to understand that world and
its hidden schemes;

What am I seeing in that seething mass, spilling a trail of thunder?
In that phosphorescence of a nocturnal sky, is my world gone
asunder?
No, it's inside my head, that has become an auditorium of wonder,
Seeing that detail of my life, a garden, a spell, that I'm now under;

Still it is not too late, that dream could have been beautiful,
A garden full of desire and foaming seas; facts that are indisputable,
I see you flutter like and injured sparrow, fleeing ecstasy,
A ballerina creating pirouettes forlornly, with no destiny;

I am driven by that darkness and silver twilight's mists,
Will I gather up the fragments of time that I have missed,
Fate has coursed its way, as flowers blooming once, now fade,
I will replenish my faith and dreams of you, without being afraid;

We have no need of words now, during these dark nights,
Engulfed in a library of desire, fate has his ways despite,
Who would join the ranks willingly and replenishing that
world of spirits,
A paradox of life that has its merits.

MAY'S START

Spring it's here, lusty, dewy and misty, laden with promise,
As the sun rises up out of its golden rim paining night's solace;
The conscious slumber does not take, as rampant beauty prevails,
Bodiless airs wafts in young treetops like shadows with no details;

Salty wind, bites my skin wrapped in that foggy air 'n which the sky hid,
Above the tree's fringed lid, I'm drawn to something beauty does
not forbid,
As ruins molder and rest unknown, but try to ascend the universe
so deep,
From those celestial vineyards, where the dim sheeted ghosts go
to sleep;

Silence pervades those moments of pleasure under those archaic trees,
Dripping moss as the wood burns it bones with a dark's smoky ease;
Upon the jet-black mirror of the lakes I see my face reflected so clear,
I will never see that forest, that's now dim and old, but still full of cheer.

May-day filled with sun and color bright, after moon's rictus and fun,
However today color is dun and those falling stars are now done;
They fell on that picket of trees hidden in the nightly dark,
They were wan and dulled by their travel, without a spark;

But Spring's ship, moving with the snow flawed winds from those
dour skies,
She has rooted and it's a resolution's firm and full of surprise, Now
trees rise with that sap ascending to their young tops
And the hawthorns boughs flowers, in a way we cannot know,

But in our homelands, they still plough the ancient way,
As Spring lingers with the goodwill that we will always endure,
that early May.

FORCE OF TIME

A trail of footsteps visible in the soft sand,
Fading in the steady wind off the drying land,
Suns fierce rays of tyrannical light, erasing all memories,
As time eat up all that's left of those boundaries;

Time's force has stripped all flesh and knowledge from the bones,
But in my head, is that alien landscape of muted tones,
A palette, of values and hues, immortal and limitless,
Imagination added to that flat bare canvas of sandy wickedness;

A sea of incessant decadence is unleased onto that blank treasure,
Of slashing brushstrokes on a cerulean sky, filled with pleasure,
Swaths of vermillion in descending arcs of sunlight,
Green and ochre where audacious lands try to show their height;

Will those memories, once lost in the carnage of my mind, return,
Will I unravel those footsteps and the imagination for which
I so yearn,
I watch with helpless dismay as sand erode the knowledge
so fair,
My vision enslaved to nocturnal ordeals that I cannot repair;

I reach for that bowl of flour, white and pure,
And lay it out in an unbroken powdered circle without allure,
To hides the slaves of nightly darkness concealed in my dreams,
Like withered branches wreathed in tortured leafy extremes;

However now that summer's here and the sun's poultice covers me,
Hiding that nightly horror with her healing spree,
Glinting of that green roiling sea folded and hiding its hollows, Waves, like a ballerina that pirouettes forlornly, I cannot follow;

But out of that water is born the promise,
In those infinite salty depths lives the desire of solace,
The future is a myth created by philosophers and dreamers,
Will I join those ranks of those wandering believers?

The truth gradually ascends to me,
As in the desert, there I am alone, with nowhere I can see,
Except for the sun's golden inferno, impossible to flee,
Allowing the future to disintegrate, while I go on to plough that final furrow.

DEW DROPS

Dew forever shining in that soft grey light,
As hope falls, while love will decay in time,
But I go where hills are built in the night,
With sun and the moon and hollows so sublime;

For there is a mystical brotherhood there,
As river and stream work out their will,
There, where love is less dear, in that misty air,
Dew forever shining with silken thread there still;

As the clouds of incense rise in that sky,
So that heavenly eyes can't see or close,
Crowns have been hurled down for eyes to cry,
I am weary of the dream-heavy prose;

      Dew forever shining in that lady's golden hair,
      And lilies are carried through many a square.

REMEMBER

The year has ended, and thrush's song has stopp'd,
Last light flows through the forests serene,
Under those ancient aspens, tall and uncropped,
As we're alone strolling amidst the green.
And we dream of those fragments of our time,
While across the horizon twilight flamed,
Sad as the night whispers those hidden rhymes,
Each of us dreaming of those words unnamed;

Writing is my destiny, to write now,
Words blazing across in that bleeding ink,
I am in this world a ghost without vow,
But passion and ambition, I should think,
Thinking of infinite depths of the mundane,
Is the sign of my deep desire, that's insane?

MEMORY

After that flaming orange and fuchsia sunset,
The night unfurls in that dark hidden forest 'twas said;

I trample on those scattered leaf's, last summer's bounty,
Disheveled bodies of her madness, displaying their color
proudly;

But as raindrops wind down the slope of a rose's petal,
It's descending onto me, released from those rosy clouds, now
changeless metal;

In my cubicle, I'm planning that perfect vacation, I do not
intent to see,
I still belongs to wherever I came from, but people do not
agree;

And I watch the scraps of paper I've scrawled my heart across,
Drift away in the wind through alleys of withered dreams,
without gloss;

I watch the courtiers, teeming with intrigues, sharing their
words,
There's no fence between decency and atrocity, a fence, yes,
but no boards;

As I still remember those diaphanous articles of lustrous silk,
so tender,
That torment my dreams during the saltiness of time and it
does not surrender.

DREAMWORLD

When I consider nature that holds everything to perfection,
While the constellation of stars have that secret influence and
connection;

I walk across the floating bridge towards my sacred world of
dreams,
Worlds of limitless imagination and soft white lilies, among
the streams;

Onto that bare canvas I smear the vivid indigo color oozing
downwards,
Descending arcs reminiscent of artillery strikes without
words;

Vermillion as bright as lust or anger, filling the valleys with
carnage.
Color bruised and punished, full of life yet discarded;

Cerulean skies, bright and azure tints engrave my imagination
filled with mayhem,
As I struggle with my canvases and the faces as I want to
portray on them;

Then sunset is swallowed by the gods and the dying sun as it
crosses the western horizon,
I return from my dreamy journey that engulfed me and wait
for the new day's rising.

THAT SANGUINE DAY

During the sanguine days of summer's splendor,
Unblemished from start to finish, they're,
Those days, that tell me, I'm the offender,
If only I knew of that timeless light, so gay;

Growth green and thirsting, spirits unfurling,
Leaf's are hungry, I desire the ardor of the sun,
Hidden in that veiling while light's whirling,
Harvesting of the ripe grapes has begun;

Plumb and round filled with promise they're,
I wonder will the vintner extract that fruity illusion,
From the trembling and yielding fruits without a scar,
With its brewing skills of transmuting and diffusion;

If I only knew those secret thoughts praised,
But night's here, the dark guillotines are raised.

SILENCE

Silence, it's in here now,
In my mind
Where thoughts are woven,
A base 'f my life.

Echoes of the past;
Hang foreboding in the air;
Spreading wide and clear,
With wings 's a chimera choir.

I try to run,
But in my mind;
Encircled by the archangel's chant,
Voices, inhuman and strange.

Silence, while chaos reigns,
Transforming bleached bones,
Drifting, in the doomed tides,
Soon bygone.

My rocks on the barren shore,
Cruelly transformed,
By sea, but silent,
Enduring my torment,
As I will indulge in dreams of summer's eternal nights.

SUMMER'S DEAD

Those storms,
Alive with leaf's,
    As if musical instruments,
Stealthy invading,
As my mind wails;

Harsh and cruel,
Wind driven and unkind,
    Grief, choking and weeping.
For that sun that once was,
Of days now so long gone;

Will that cradling wind,
Waving those boughs afar,
    With indifference 'n mind,
And sit on its throne,
Enfolding long dead leaf's;

He has taken them away,
His indigo color filled sky,
    that once held a sun-gilded air.
now just a dead grace,
and horizons fill'd with dreamy hues;

Shattered songs of winter's tale,
with indifference, they sing,
    Of Summer's time graceless dead,
And her eternal soul,
Filled with color, now gone.

MORNING

Morning looms…;
I cannot stop it,
It's dawn, I must presume,
    I dread, of which I can't quit;

But later, before tonight,
I'll hide from all those threats,
Concealed from that early light,
    Shrouding my body from morn's besets;

Maybe it's an early dawn,
As I hide in my cocoon,
I notice that the morn is now fully drawn,
    It's surreptitious purpose, is hiding till noon;

So, what do I say?
Maybe I'm not fair,
That dawn, it will not go away,
    They say humanity does not care!

But now I am fully awake,
A dream, stretching, realizing the day's light has arrived,
On wings I float , wondering shall I partake?
    As my life is an endless song, that I must survive;

Alive, trying, but to find I'm apart,
    Inside the ruins of my heart.

THOUGHTS

There is a light shining in my mind, cold and devoid of the norm,
Images inside my mind are black, as light is spiritual and misty;
    I have no preconception of things that are without form,
    I have looked at it long and hard, but it all remains wispy.

This is not an easy time when Winter is coming, without the sunny light,
As I look at those empty bottles glittering, after night's darkness,
    There are places I have never seen, during that night,
    Steeling myself with a sheen, to accept the stars harshness;

Stars that shine with a fluidness that're like pillars of light,
Their haloed lightness just visible in my mind,
    Alas, I let that white light wither, to shown color in spite,
    Those immortal colors more than every hue I did ever grind;

A brushstroke of vivid indigo oozing down,
Decadence of my mind unleased,
    Slashing orange and brown,
    Cerulean color, prevailing shapes are seized;

But softness in highlights is retained, full of insolence,
Audacious and proud they're as a revolution uncontrolled,
    As waves at the "cote d'ivoire" incessant and full of innocence,
    My mind covers the canvas with ideas that unfold.

But in my mind that sea of colors and form is an empty canvas,
An ancient battlefield covered by the indigo storm clouds all around,
    Now that once empty field, full of waiting bodies, there to enchant us,
    As my paint enshroud that canvas with colors I did found.

LOVE LOST

Love, a word full of color and lights,
But winter can come with its naked wet trees and cold nights,

A solitaire yew's finger points upwards, despite,
As I try to stand up, from that furnace of arid ground I need
to fight,

Unable, as I am an organic part of that universe unknown,
I seek the language of the cosmos, that poets use and hone,

But during the nights, that follows suns reign,
I look at that universe, a pond of cosmic terror and pain,

Losing that universe, that was once so full of vigor,
Now a dark place, doomed, and not getting bigger,

And rooted there, but we do forget those kisses, tender and brief,
All that is left now is the barren yew tree's sheaf's,

While her footsteps fade in that yellow sand,
I quietly brush away their secrets, hidden in that soft land.

SINERALITY

Sun emerges as she pulls, twists and tears,
Releasing its wild inferno on us,
Searching for the genesis it so fears,
But as morning looms that sun rises thus;

The vision that's left, so full of beauty,
A universe full with cosmic terror,
Stars shining and doing their divine duty
In that space full of heresy and error;

After suns crowning glory it sinks in gloom,
Horizon's brooding dark and forbidden,
Night comes soon, born out of heavens dark womb,
Feuding, sun's daily glory, now hidden;

But within nights wisps, beauty is brooding,
As my left hand illustrates what is eluding.

WORDS

We have no need for words as they are an illusion,
I am engulfed in my dreams during those tenebrous hours of
my confusion;

> Symbol of my madness while my world evaporates in
> meaningless time,
> A world of tinted glass, burned and brown, shades I find
> so sublime;

I am hiding behind the proscenium, unseen and silent hiding
my mind,
As I am looking into that mirror, trying to understand what
those rhymes defined;

> While at the misty seashore, my thoughts disintegrate
> like sand,
> And they'll scatter by those saline winds, I cannot feel
> or understand;

While darkness descends, midnight surrenders its magic light,
And the nocturnal sky with his thousands of wrathful stars of
the night, complain;

> Summer has ended with its golden glory, love and lust,
> While those stars think of the kisses, tender and brief;

While I am troubled in numerous ways,
I hanker for the smiles we shared during those secret days.

CAT

Outside the window there was a black cat,
Looking at me in fear, as I stared,
It was in my dream, I saw where it sat,
A thing conjured out of fear we shared;

A creature sleeking in the nightly darkness,
Ancient's tyrants, of the world we live in,
Sensing, the hidden places and stillness,
Of things that're secret, and I wouldn't know.

Connived they're with skills that I didn't see,
And words enter my mind in slow chanter,
What naughty tricks has it put upon me,
I am talking, hoping to enchant her.

That cat with a voice consorting twilight,
Out, at the window in moons gold skylight.

TWICE

As we sat together that autumn's evening,
The last berries are dripping with rain, as if grieving;
    And in the hourglass's pieces fall, spilling down so sublime,
    Yet if it does not seem a moment's, of my time;

That I wrote those words,
As I had a thought for none but birds;
    And in the trembling cerulean color of the nightly sky,
    Was the moon, now worn down, although no one knows
    why;

In the darkness, past radiance of light that once was above,
We sat quietly at the name of love;
    Thinking of our desires and experiences fused,
    Waiting for next day's sepia luminosity to appear still
    bruised;

While the new day is like a winding ancient stair,
Leading to that crumbling roof in need of repair;
    But summer is over now all's left but the razor-keen air,
    An edge like broken glass not blunted by time and wear;

Winters's hidden awhile and masked by hood and cloak,
Life is draining from the soil, floating away like smoke;

WOODLAND PATH

The autumn season is here, with her mature beauty and
clammy surprises,
As under the soft sunlight, rivers mirror the clouds that are rising;
    I walk that woodland path filled with fluttering leaf's,
    And see the harvest, full of ripeness and fruits filled to
    the eaves;
That sweet kernel and plump hazel shells, unshackled apples
are still there,
I watch that enchanted golden stubble field dying in the
cooling air;
    But inside me dwells that dark thought of autumn's
    latest form,
    Who can fathom its depth and appetite for rain and storm?
Upon the brimming water, I see the soft-dying day,
The last crickets sing their soft mourn, with voices once so gay;
    Golden leaf's drift in the still water,
    Mysterious, and beautiful, heading for the places they'll
    gather;
A signal of the end to ending,
    As wind arrives on her clamorous wings and trees know
    what it's sending,
    I watch from behind my fortification peering at the enemy;

Knowing the assault is coming, encircling me without serenity,
Birds once joyful, brimming with life, are gone from the skies,
Swallows flown away from this vale, unseen by my eyes.

STORM

When I consider nature that holds everything to perfection,
While the constellation of stars have that secret influence and
connection;

But, as I live in that land of sun, winters drizzle and chill,
immeasurably mired, with muddy roads that probably have
drunk their fill;

In this land of damp forested hills, birds sing,
Music in that sweet air that autumn sometimes will bring;

The great harvest's finished,
With thousands of fruits to pick, cherished with love undiminished;

The sky hides those high mountains,
Of uncharted beauty where rivers are spouting water like fountains;

Within my forested wild land, storm clouds gather,
Winds push that water aflutter with blather;

The last field flowers are crushed on wet boughs curved and dank,
While bird's bruit their song forlornly, without a thank;

The water wheel with its warped decaying timbers struggles,
As the dark forests debate their incantation and trees buckle;

Under those storm laden skies wind strike with it cruel whip,
Its wrath and avarice know as it holds the hills and forest in its grip;

Autumn has arrived with its profoundest intimate cruelty,
In its desire of power and carnage, it's often without beauty;

THE PAINTER

Hidden in old age, is the root,
A face of where we all once stood;
> But those days are all gone,
> The bugle is now silent, and we're all alone;
Memories leaning backward with their lipless grins,
They are the bones, that were beneath the palest of the skins;
> As, I am a painter of the olden school,
> Still using gesso to begin, pretending it's cool;
Winter's day is settling down, withered leaf's wheeling at my feet,
Snowy showers are there for me to beat;
> Conscious comes in the mornings, like waves kneeling
> deep,
> Unbeknown of what their mothers did reap,
I watch those dreams that enthralled me,
The first coat is drying, as I decide what's next to be;
> As I wait in my darkest moods, that will clear soon,
> Enchained visions of mine mingled, that's a blessed boon!
While I am guileless and pondering,
I'll go on with my pointless colorful wandering;
> The mist of winter screens my sights, wondering about
> what's next to be, or might,
> Yes, while I stand there to decide, is that color really right?
I am playing that exquisite nocturne of my imagination,
Applying those luminal colors, with hesitation

ANGER

Wings of colored glass are rapidly beating,
A seething mass of rage during the night;
Soon we'll see these lands without competing,
Places on which blood fell during the fight;

Ancient fens, like keyboards over which hands dance,
Playing that sad tune of things now forgotten;
Anger recedes and morning breaks and advances,
While the moon fades, as if misbegotten;

Autumn, oft chilly exist in many incarnations,
In the fen, I sit under that ancient rowan tree;
And think of those blooms, all land's creations,
Summer is waning, times I could not foresee;

And thus, in those very lands I know so well,
I dwell there amid those rowan leaf's.

OTHER LANDS

Those branches, leaf's and blossoms I have seen,
Within the fen covered with dew, still and clean,

I follow that path obscure and now alone,
A way haunted by ill angels and shadows unbeknown,

Towards my home, in the long vales filled with endless floods,
I have reached those new lands as 'twas in my blood,

Filled with wild and strange climes and mountains supreme,
Chasms, and caves, titanic woods and forms only I can see, it seems,

At morn, twilight dim, clouds obscuring my vision bright,
Hoping for future's radiant smile and sweet hope that will be
soon my sight,

I have followed seas without shore, where restless winds aspire,
Now in lands anew, and memories unknown, I wait on slopes
verdant, without ire,

I dream of moment to which, I wish, the sun dawned behind
the trees in the north,
In that golden light that tease and flout reality, to which my
spirit simple stands forth,
Against the uttermost of the earth and fate, which I hated so,
of late,

While I fight earths un-honored things, and clime's striking
errands great,

These things are in vain, in this foreign land of mine,
As those woe are not earthy woe, neither is clime to blame,
when it did not shine.

MUSINGS

Our souls' lives in the moonlit night and landscapes fair,
Waiting for the golden sunrise, it's dear radiance so tender
and clear,
Dew is done and grass all mown, while flowers wither, some
do sleep,
There is no need for sinuous words and illusions we all keep;

Engulfed in that tenuous fabric of desire,
I follow that enchanted path, I have acquired,
While others are sleeping, I watch hazel leaf's die,
Winter is approaching, full of ache and a dark skies;

Leaf's, golden and dry are now dead on that barren ground,
I gather them from where they fell, so profound,
But that golden sun has arrived, retarded in that gentle mist,
It will make the day seem less brief and showed what we
missed;

Now the memories of landscapes fair have grown dim,
As the nocturnal sky has left us, and sun's golden rays engulf
worlds rim,
Losing oneself in a wordless understanding of desire,
Beside the golden leaf's and withered flowers in that land I
so require.

SUNLIGHT

The flower's perfume, pure and light,
Rosé light of the sun's last words during evening's fray;
Songs that I once hummed, I must now write during the night,
In that once heard sound, 'mid my thoughts the treasures
must lay;

But the triumphant sun will rise again in that autumn sky,
pale and rose,
With the chant of approaching choirs, and morning's sweet
flight,
The living strains of flames that we all seek and chose,
The light of sun turns white, scattering those nocturnal dyes
in morning's light;

That daily beauty, my mistress and a morning's rose,
Nothing stirs in that forest air, like cloud on cloud, leaf on leaf,
In a sea of silence, I compose those crystalline rhymes, no
one knows,
It's but a dream within a dream, of beauty, which I do not
belief;

But once again evening will descend, violating my solitude,
As I grieve for days demise and sun's rosy fall;
But like a loyal soldier I will stand till sunrise and its colorful
prelude,
Then I do not dwell with streaming eyes but will rejoice
instead.

WINTERS FIRST DAY

Snow has landed in the groves that I have been,
Gone is the sultry breath of the summer's day, that I've seen,
Tender hands gone pale and cold dur'ng that day,
The last of autumn's leaf's, 're still golden, now crumpled
where they lay;

Moving like a trail of fading footsteps by that cold windy sky,
A memory of things unseen, unraveled and now dry,
Summer has dwindled away, and flowers recede and die,
The memory of unfulfilled promises makes me often cry;

All that remains is the dream, that is no longer a dream,
Vanished into the cruelties of time and winters regime,
Hidden in that silver twilight mists, barely seen,
Summer betrayed, by broken vows, we've forgotten 'twas so
sublime;

My mind floats but my memories 're aglow,
And my brow folds in wrinkled gloom seeing the snow,
Thinking of storms that will come with masses of clouds that
bloom,
Trembling hills within that rising mist are now full of doom;

I hanker for that morning's light, the mystic link of th't flower
gold,
Waiting for that rosy light 'twas yesterday's delight I am told,
Now earth is white and bare, like a grave that's gone cold
dur'ng the night,
While trees silently toss, with no pleasure or song dur'ng their
sad plight;

ÉRIU

I lived once in a dream-laden land filled with clouds and
mysteries,
With love tales woven into the fabric of time and history;

Roses, once seen into ladies' hair, now fading,
As dew sinks into the earth, kings die, and armies gone
a raid'ng;

In my dream-awakened eyes I see horsemen fall and cry,
An unknown perishing army, lands at those windy shores
ready to die;

Will that dove-grey faery land still exist,
Queens, kings and armies fight with glimmering hands
that no one c'n resist;

While lands are overthrown by a woman's glance,
I labor to build the story of perfect beauty, rhyme and stance;

Although from you I derive all this mischance,
To dwell with streaming eyes looking at history, without
interference;

I weep, by the soft song of the rain,
A song sung by drops falling on the trees, as if in pain;

My heart suffers to live without joy or woe,
I left that grey land of strive, and beauty 'twas long ago.

DAYBREAK

I love that mystic light that'll appears soon,
But I dread that light there yonder, in heaven,
Weak is that gleam on that far hill I've seen,
Have I drawn those glances of that rising sun?

Prodigious chaos, reins in my life now,
Life in the green valleys and glens, laid low;
I've left the dark blue open sea, I've loved,
Yet, I remain near to that ocean pure;

The fair light of heavens unclosed gate falls,
Golden and warm, a blessing at early dawn,
The glittering scales of the rising sun anew,
Above that misty line of rowans great,

Claws knotted tight and gnarled feet 'neath rocks,
As those boughs, rock in the early morning's breeze,
Savage beauty under that green velvet screen,
As that gate closes and night's running near;

SUNSET

That sunset so glorious as if a dream,
The day's end with its last happy beam,
As sun relinquish day to moons soft light,
Night makes firm her dark domain in spite;

Will I catch those last rays before flames die?
Or will sun's final golden glow pass me by,
As darkness falls, I watch the birth of stars,
And moon's pale enchantment show's nature's scars;

We look at heaven we'll think of eternity,
As I build my faery palace full of absurdity,
I see towers, spars against that dark sky,
As smoke rises above towns not knowing why;

Did I pursue that fading god in vain,
As I write this verse without anger or pain.

DREAMS

My dream did weave darkness and shadows strong,
I have that bitter knowledge many wanderers have had for long,
Walking on the sands at beach's verge, a dream to pursue,
Along ocean's edge with waters wild and blue;

Caverns filled with saline waters clear and so unmet,
I could have gone to my eternal rest, among lifting winds, I can't forget,
But I live in that strange east land so dim,
I was troubled, bewildered not knowing the road was that grim;

I move over many a tangled spray, tripping as I try,
Resignedly beneath the deep sky where the melancholy of waters lie,
That sky dewy and dim by the mountains and the river murmuring lowly,
Those grey woods by that swamp where frogs and snails move slowly.

BELLS

Hear those silvery bells within that icy winter's air,
Merriment and fun during that starry night, so fair,
A crystalline night with bells that musically wells,
But, now, in that cold air, their turbulence tells!

While heaven seems to twinkle with a stars sprinkle,
I think of bells melancholic meaning and tone that sinks and
tinkle
While that sound floats clear, despite their rusty throats,
I feel the glory in that muffled rolling and bright notes;

But while I sit in that ghoul haunted glade, that dim and sober,
Hearing those bright bells as I wait for dawn's coming ever closer,
Then I see those roses so white, rise up in that dark glade,
Making that meadow in early sunrise abrade and fade;

> As those bells sound their harmony that their melody
> foretells,
> And that nebulous luster is reborn within the dell.

MEMORIES OF CONTRAST

I remember standing in that dell seeing those virgin rose's
so pure,
As they bath in early sun's light that's iridescent but demure,

While I rest, within that silent grove, where tree's claws ar'
knotted tight,
And untroubled by that dark stand, and the ancient blight;

Incarnations I discard, as autumn abandon's summer's folly,
Leaf's crumple, losing their mirth, and 're replaced by melancholy,

In my memories I see cruelty in the wrongs I have' suffered,
Wrongs conveniently forgotten, and well covered up;

I am not the one that opens the door to a soul,
That door will lead to hell within that sleeping grove's knoll,

But with sun's incongruous light, oft lacking those colors,
The sun's ambience light, which I need and control to make
that sun guileful;

In my dream oaks and forests, speak to me when lit by those
sun's rays,
Hiding my secrets of those ideas that I did not appraise in
any ways.

LEAF'S

The autumn's season is back,
While the forest puts on her red dress,
In the light of the autumn,
With its golden sunlight,
I filled my basket,
With pretty leaf's of the path,
And the acorns that fall on the moss,
Where rabbits dance in circles.
And mice having great feasts,
While the mushrooms grow.
Ah! that life is sweet, so sweet,
Autumn's azure coat is strewn with many stars,
While during the agitation of old gnarled trees,
The autumn's season is back.

AUTUMN

Those golden leaf's, dry, but playful of late,
I breathe that spicy scent of autumn's fiery breeze,
And remember the summer's secrets, we did create,
Will that harvest moon still shimmer in those now barren trees;

While sun's rosy color has now faded, and is less defined,
We sleep in the birch and hemlock grove, with those dreams
we can't unlock,
As those crumpled leaf's tumble round in that wispy wind of
which they're twined,
While tree's gnarled feet are firmly planted 'neath that ancient
stony rock;

As spiders capture life in their silvery tissue, carefully suspended,
Crickets sing their final song of their impending doom, We
know summer's glory has finally ended,
And autumn's ancient wonder is in full bloom;

With storm's fury and natures feared striking light, We have
spells and wards that are so often cast,
Its nature's glory; that oft is a blight,
God's and nature's power are unknown, great and vast;

IMAGE

Far above the tranquil seas, and the valleys where kings still reign,
Filled with mountains, forests, clouds, and that gentle rain,
Beyond the confines of the starry skies,
My spirit roams with agility after that golden sunrise;

I loathe that morbid miasma my life once was,
Those fragments of forgotten time gone, reflecting in that glass,
Across it's eclipsed azure horizon lit by dying sun,
I think of those mundane thoughts, that I've done;

Nor the white crocus's dreams of her final demise heat the
summer brings,
It's the perennial and annihilating thirst to create, to distil
and purify things,
I ardently desire to transform dreams of polyhedral trees onto
paper so clear,
An endless forest of green beauty 'cross an eclipsed horizon,
and disappear;

IMAGINATION

In those tranquil valleys, where kings still reign,
Filled with mountains, forests, and gentle brooks,
Beyond the confined night's starry domain,
My spirit roams, wanting sun's golden looks;

I loathe that morbid miasma my life once was,
Those fragments of forgotten light gone by,
Past the azure horizon just because,
Thinking of those mundane thoughts, during the night;

Nor of the white crocus's silent demise,
It's my perennial thirst to create,
The ardent desire to transform, revise,
Create green beauty 'cross the horizon's fate;

　　　Roses throb and die in the bygone days,
　　　Days gone, as sunlight dies on that rosy way.

WINTER HAS ARRIVED

Dark birds, without soul, utter their jarring cries,
Destroying summer's hidden memories;

> Autumn's light, gold'n and aged smiles and lies,
> Brooding in that dark forest of reveries;

With that impatient wind, fill'd with grief,
The silent summer's light now hidd'n and weep'ng;

> Once sultry and splendid, t'was sun's belief,
> Now sallow, as it peers at her dank reapin';

Summer dies by degrees, t'was here too brief,
Her mantle, azure sown with stars sleepin';

> Her eternal soul and graceless death hidd'n,
> Among the thinning gold'n leaf's of those trees,

Winter approaches, lakes cold and forbidden,
White robed forms fall 'n agony and freeze;

> Winter has arriv'd it's weary snow's hidden,
> I'll close the doors and windows with unease;

And build my faery castle unbidden,
Then I will dream 'f the blue horizons hidden.

CHANGING TIMES

Leaf's free of their branches,
Floating in the frigid breeze;
    I see the bleak silhouettes to the bare oak trees,
    Their sinister branches twisted 'n semblances of agony
    in the cooling wind;
Color is fading like endnotes of a score,
Crumpled leaf's are still playing the'r golden tune;
    Whispering their swinging air,
    Swirling and floating 'round me in a playful way;
The magic of the moment beautiful and gay,
I witness the season change the metamorphosis of times;
    Shadowy clouds gather at the horizon,
    Heralding the conclusion of summer;
The last of the azure sky 's swallowed up,
Leaving me with my bitter dreams.
    But soon we will plunge ourselves into the icy shadows,
    And summer's stunn'ng afternoons will be gone;
Yes, I already hear the dead thuds of logs below,
Falling on the cobblestones and the dying grass below,
    All of winter's stony bareness will return soon.

HIDDEN

As I wander along that hidden crook'd path,
Seeing those beasts, with their deep gold'n eyes;
Waiting for their prey, with fierce and proud stance,
Men have trampl'd this path with awe created guise;

Along with their carts and their huddl'd prizes,
As crickets watch them pass redoubl'ng their song,
And duck and drake hide in reeds, were it 'rises,
I take pity of those beasts suffer'ng so long;

Black anger is veil'd in earthly paradise,
I try to chase away their mocking nightmares,
But it's weary, nature does despise me,
Thru that wild forest, rustling as night wears;

I gazed around those boughs with'n eagle's eye,
Stand'ng upon those rocks and frown at those dark clouds,
I try to understand what I'm seeing and why,
But it hidden in darkness that's it enshrouds.

DREAM WITHIN DREAM

Much did I see in this world so trivial,
The inside of my skull became an auditorium,
An abstract fantasyland, a ruin of ancient beauty,
A forest with ragged elms and thorns innumerable;

Will I wake up with master's knowledge or hand?
But no, I am lost in that labyrinth I have made,
A life filled with half-images and half-written pages,
But I can dream, and I've toiled hard of late;

To leave those monuments behind,
Let the young faces play whatever tricks they will,
My painter's brush consumes their dreams and past,
While I live under that azure sky and golden sunlight;

I still dream of that enchanted isle in that tumultuous sea,
But it is a dream within a dream,
While I wait for that dark tide that autumns so admires,
Within the encircling horizon drenched in tyrannical light.

WINTER'S APPROACH

Summer's now past, days prove ominous,
The year has gone stale and has now faded,
Full of unborn fulfillments and those forgotten promises,
Frost descends during the nightly air, covering the color that
summer created;

Life is gone in hiding, leaving the soil, as silence rises,
Wind's gathering it's strength, but daylight dwindles,
Dreams 're hidden in that silvery mist, the one the night's disguises,
A horizon that was distant once, now cold and brittle;

Summer's dark carcass now kissed by winter's pale moon,
Gone are those vast nebulas of foliage,
And the luminous crystal pyramids of summer's light during noon,
The future is a myth, a desire of philosophers, without knowledge;

As night retire of her nightly reign,
Seasons dance their own wild palette of color,
Decadence unleashed in regular stages and design,
The summer's green strokes have grown duller;

Winters white bouquet, fills those empty spaces,
A world of narrow imagination and hues has appeared,
Full of insolence and indifference of life wasted,
Sunrise's dun light sinks away as feared;

Winter sits still on its icy throne,
Dreaming of those dark restless chilly ones,
Refusing to let the sun be reborn and reclaim her brightness
that shone,
But chaos will be defeated as the solar vessel ascents the
realm, winter shuns.

WINTER

That worn water wheel, crumpled after decades of wear,
Unable to turn in that morbid dark water it was once so clear;

> The last offerings of autumn are now faded and dry,
> While the grim wooden cabin's door is standing awry;

It's unable to withstand winter's ragged hand,
While the dark forests hover in that silver' and misty land;

> While gnarled branches catch those broken wisps of clouds,
> We'll wait as the brave day to sinks in that silent night
> it's enshrouds;

Silence 's surrounded by drizzling snow, wherever it falls,
Ravaging land and countryside, eerily embracing winter's call;

> Notice the strange unease that's crept in the earth,
> Light 's now conferred only in a sulphureous dream of
> her rebirth;

While withered trees are undulated in tortured forms,
As outstretched arms reaching for those coming storms;

> My environment's metamorphosed into a chimera of
> winter's world,
> Sun's longing beams are unable to penetrate black
> clouds that're still furled;

But there is beauty in those nocturnal dreams,
And winter's crystalline white blanket hides all its cunning
schemes.

ANGELS

That harvest moon sailing unruffled in evening's sky,
I meander on those obscure pathways, knowing summer's gone;
> It is not a thing done, and I see figures prowling as I pass by,
> Nameless mystical things hiding in that mist, colorless
> and drawn;

This lonely path I walk, haunted by ill angels, to reach my
lands far,
Lands with bottomless vales and boundless gray seas;
> Trees with dew dripping, grey and wet, under gloomy
> skies without a star,
> Alas, summer has departed with memories of those
> radiant hours of ease;

Now winter reign's those once verdant slopes with a chilly
insanity,
Transforming those memories of departed bliss into white
cold bastions;
> Storms raging over that bleak land with its dark cloud
> canopy,
> Domains, orphans and unfathered fruits are now barren
> on mute pastures;

Seeing that weakening of day's golden eye, without joy,
Storm's last fury has gone, and fields have dried;
There is no cause for caroling under the winter's ploy,
Now that land's features have shrunk, and its future denied.

DREAMING OF WINTER

Season's pass till autumn fades and rest;
Heavens bring thoughts of eternity not seen,
Then comes winter where autumn has been,
Building the palaces in ways he knows best;

I dream of skies blue, clear and undressed,
And softly, through the mist, I'll watch unseen,
As see threads of smoke rise above the scene,
The start of that greedy, cruel, winter's quest;

But winter's season is asleep cold and brief,
While sweet summer looks on, waiting for her turn,
To carry peace and care to humans will,
While winter's veil enfolds, claiming her fief;

But hope arises, with the sun's return;
As the moon pours her pale enchantment still.

SUMMER'S HAS BEEN HERE

In those meadows, mature but still green, I wait,
Time runs slow when waiting for sun to set,
We know that summer has been here, of late;

The time has come when orchards abate,
With appl' and pear trees fruit's rich and ripe,
In those meadows, mature but still green, I wait;

Much have I travelled during summer's golden fate,
And written of times that only bards still know;
We know summer is here, yes late;

In that morn with leaf's blown dry and gold,
I know autumn is gone, winter sets in,
In those meadows, mature but still green, I wait,

Nature dies in frost that winter will create,
It's all hidden by that snowy layer,
As summer is again so very late;

But, remember that gentle summer fete,
With many a warm sweep, whirling around,
In those meadows, mature but still green, I wait.

DESCENDING INTO CHAOS

As she softly descended the stairway;
Billowing clouds passed the window on that quiet day,
Without a noise, she seems to dance wherever she was seen,
Her wings of colored glass spread wide like a faery queen;

Hidden is the real drama, and it's sad depths;
Passions like dark figures walking with those silent steps;
I am looking in a mirror, and try to understand of what is there,
While Moons has filled the chamber with phosphorescent air;

A luminous poison, unbeknown and invisible to my eyes,
A dance to the waving cadence of lies;
With eyes each one watching me, aware of that secret plot,
Yes, I have been wounded during my nocturnal caress.

By that sea, that immense' green ungovernable excess,
Comprised of multitudinous saline waters, gathering without
finesse;
The woman I will never again, see or know,
A sinister flower bearing the incense of so long ago;

The melancholy waters lie beneath the dark sky as it advances,
While all my days I live within those endless unknown trances.

DREAMS AND DOOM

So fair is that sun when it's lowers 'n flames from above,
It is full of joy, happiness and love;
But now's the end her daily life, glorious warmth and
the dreams it behoves;
I have seen those gold'n beams, with flowers and
streams, in glades and warm coves;
Alas, light departs, pursuing that fading god, after its daily quest;

The last sun's rays tremble on aspen's twigs' crest;
Ready to depart, but isn't yet mature;
Unable to escape the darkness, knowing that it can't endure
Light vignetted and her beauty captured but outworn, as
night approaches.

Those golden eves, when all the world reposes,
It's time of darkness, dreams and doom;
Night grip is firm in his somber and dark domain;
While the moon pours down the enchantment, she has amassed;

Soft and golden she was, gone now is that wan face of many
'n hour past;
So fair was that sun, when it did lowers in flames from
above.

THE SKY IN AUTUMN

That pale sky of autumn, soft and golden,
  Your lips morose, with words it can't behold,
    And memories of days that were foretold,
      In my dreams, I'll see those stories of old;

Filled with sorrow and much regret,
  Silently we watch that sky where we met,
    The birth of stars and views we can't forget,
      And hear the singing of a mortal quartet;

Sinless tunes with that innocent touch;
  In that enchanted light we love so much,
    We wait for winter and his chilly clutch,
      While under those yews we will build our hutch;

Winter sits in silent and solemn state,
  To watch sun's fading light, and her final fate,
    The nightly shades assume their state,
      As I sleep in a faery palace great.

THE LANDSCAPE OF MY MIND

That sun, hot, in a sky so clear and blue,
Flowers 're dreaming and dancing in the breeze
Sun's gilded air and nature's soft dreamy hue;

Cerulean blue enfolding nature true,
When I'm surrounded by the forest of trees,
That sun, hot, in a sky so clear and blue;

Descending are these past memories or two,
Horizons, of colors that I want to seize,
Sun's gilded air and nature's soft dreamy hue;

In the silence of summer's early revue,
And sun's sweet air, flowers will rise with ease,
That sun, hot, in a sky so clear and blue;

Beauty of mornings time has come anew,
Gone is winters hard face and cold breeze,
Sun's gilded air and nature's soft dreamy hue;

But summer's warmth will soon end her view,
Creeping she comes o'er that faded moon's light,
Full of uncertain ghosts that're chilly and undue,
Sun's gilded air and nature's soft dreamy hue;

ASHEN LANDS

Ashen is that land where plants
  And green foliage wouldn't grow,
A place silent and sad, without the color,
  That' nature's normally does bestow;

The sky, grey and swollen,
  Hiding the full moon as it advances,
Wild, lascivious spirits are hidden,
  Behind those gnarled branches there,
As they try to catch those broken,
  Wisps of the clouds in that dank sky,
And are throwing out those,
  Wandering shadows, that I do decry;

While I take courage,
  At the sight of that oft hidden moon,
Hiding in shadows,
  And playing with winds tall after noon,
And we set forth with our thoughts aflame,
  And hearts overladen,
Walking that dark path in that ashen plain,
  Barren, and not of nature's creation,
Gone is that universal ecstasy of that loving sun,
  Nature's life is drifting into a deep slumber,
As summer is done;

The sages of olden times believed
  That destiny is written on scripts here;
But those destinies are ancient now,
  As magic books make it clear on the pages I peer;
But this darkness will not last
  As the ploughed land of my dreams 's recast,
And summer's vast empire hangs over the tables of nature,
  When new light is cast into those hives of color of the past.

THE HUNT

Remember those days, now well away,
Of times that were, but wouldn't stay,
    Those well-trodden paths under a cloudy pall,
    And those whispering aspen, awaiting sun's fall;

The hunting bugle is no more,
Neither is that toned shrill, as from before,
    And in the heath and up that hill,
    Amidst the dense forest where foliage 'ts so still;

The hunter waits, hidden in his turfed grave,
Midst mists, chills and all that the season gave,
    Waiting for its quarry within the vines loaded runs,
    As it reaps that sweet fruit, kissed by that maturing Sun;

He waits as the hours are oozing and light's waning,
The deer appears, leaping and defying hunter training;
    While clouds bloom, and that day softly dies,
    A choir the gnats mourn the hunter's demise;

But we may never behold beneath a darkened gloom,
That beloved deer, crossing the rippling flume,
    Till we think of those warm days that will never cease,
    And the sinking of the sun that lives until the end of
    its lease.

THUNDERSTORM

I see that undulating mass of rage and grief,
Those dark churning clouds wild and massif;

> Hiding that sun, tranquil, gentle and gold,
> But now colliding with thunder of old;

Intermingling with a world without release,
Heaven has turned to blood, bleeding for peace;

> I dream of grotesque angels descending,
> Roaring as they strike the earth without ending;

Sending up plumes of flame and dark smoke,
When glimmers show in that nocturnal cloak;

> And so, invisible to those birds circling overhead,
> Among the celestial vineyards ready but now dead.

FLOWERS

I wandered in the bliss of solitude,
Through the scrub, lush and verdant, 'n that soft air,
A host of flowers, their color a fortitude,
Heads fluttering in the breeze, strong and fair;

Thousands I saw there in a single glance,
A riot of bright yellow sparkling with glee;
While I floated in that day's bliss, perchance,
But above those flowers, darkness I see;

A glimmer of night flickers in the sky,
Forests and mountains slowly hide from me,
Lulled by enchantment those flowers will die,
But voice in the scented nigh sings, while they flee;

When flower's color is distilled, at night' meets,
As their feet die, their body still lives sweet.

EPILOGUE

Now that the sun-gilded air has cooled,
And nature has shortened her wan light,
The last flowers nod knowing they are fooled,
Enfolded by that cradling wind they can't fight;

Night falls, its azure coat, sown with many a star,
A mantle of chilling grace and driven winds,
In the vales, boughs hide in shadows bizarre,
Nature dies until nothing more we can find;

Welcome that time of winds and unkind light,
Summer's book is closed, its slate wiped,
My poems withered before I could write,
I hold inspiration while nature gripped;

But sun will return and winters defeat,
With the gilded warm light of summer sweet.

MEADOWS GREEN

In those rich days, clouds encircle my lien,
That radiant queen her day's journey's done,
>   Her glimmering wings have that radiant sheen,
>   While meadows green still sparkle after rains won;

While I compose songs that mortals can't hear,
They're harmonies ripe and sweet in tone,
>   While the glow of summer fade and light 's dear,
>   Days colored crimson filled with leaf's, wind-blown;

Days 're clear, like mountain streams fast and deep,
Then autumn winds sweep in with their chilly touch,
>   And boughs in that glade have a silvery sheen,
>   Gone are those summer's eves of memories past;

But the spirits which my dreams inspire hide,
During those beauteous winter's evening skies.

JANUARY

That January, cold unkind and full of grief,
Bare trees alone and empty with not a single leaf;

Today's winds are wild, with a chill that's unfair,
While black ravens call, in winter's cooling air;

Snake-like thorny brambles twists and creep,
Sparrows on daring wings seek the last fruit' to reap;

While they complain, when pecking in their greed,
Trees do thrive on the desolation they all need;

Gone now is that lace of summers pleasure,
Not a memento left for us to treasure;

Trees have released their last leaf's at break of day,
Joining the others, now blown far away;

The wan sun is hidden behind that misty veil,
Lighting that enchanted land of mornings pale;

But after those leaf's are burnt with frost,
And the last fruit is now fully lost;

The dark days will soon be less brief,
And tuft of flowers will be shown, hiding our grief.

NATURES GLAMOUR

While I drink that sweet wine,
In the morn's break of the day,
I wait with parched lips, as if a shrine,
To see that sun's banner red and gay;

I will forget those drops in anguish,
Those in the past and the future I will see,
That sun's scalding I cannot banish,
When I dwell beneath that ancient tree;

Weeping in that sunny day,
As night has worn and turned into morn,
I cannot control its starry decay,
While I live in desolation so forlorn;

While day's winds have grown wearied,
Warring on that barren rocky beach,
While that saline tableau awaits to be refereed,
By those winds so mighty in their reach;

But with the rich beauty of summer's night,
After day's wild displays and clamor,
I rest and savor that last wine, as I might,
While everything is still, nature is now without glamour;

MOODS

O' why that mockery, love is part of life,
It fills the heart with fire and flames so full,
    But as my ancestors now lie in those fields wide and green,
    I muse while my heart murmurs; O' you moldering body,
But no, forget that body, life fires the soul,
I would not exchange it, for my fields and forests deep,
    I am no longer that shepherd in meadows past,
    Not singing on my way but musing silently;
When I sit on that porch-way now cool,
And the ruddy lights fade's away,
    Shadows shoot across that field,
    And yet that light and giddy souls of cavaliers are still there,
I linger when darkness deepens;
Gone now is that summer's lace and those gallant gentlemen,
    With their gay and glittering talk and amorous songs,
    Now my days become more plaintive and paler,
Whence I escape to lives breezes and stormy quakes;
And I find ever saying: yes, I'm content!

PENDING DOOM

On that soft summers' morn, I stood upon that woody hill, I
saw that shorn field, a naked pasture 'twas.
I played once in that grassy plain, now long gone and very still,
Land bereft, before the sun rose, without a pause;

> The road too, is forlorn, with none of those daily prints,
> along with those last flowers, now too wet to bloom.
> Soil washed away leaving only those stony jewels glints,
> The songs of the forests gone, crushed by approaching doom;

Frolicking birds once happy, have now less to say,
I hide beside those boughs, glistening, wet and dank.
Rain, coming, drops aflutter in this windy day,
They will all gather on tree's wizened bark;

> Across the forest I see a window alight,
> That's where the flowers were, before they bloomed,
> Past that fen and barren fields, I did run to that place
> so bright,
> But the wind worked against me and the road was
> ungroomed;

The trees beside were unclad, shorn naked, by wind and rain,
Will I reach that garden path, once smooth and neat.
The last flower chalices still shown, that wind and rain
couldn't slain,
While the trees yellowing leaf's fly like lace unraveled and
incomplete;

> I'm tired and dusty after roaming for that reassuring light,
> They would not find me changed, with that pending doom,
> Only more sure of all things that are true in the land
> filled with fright,
> As I know how to set forth on that path hidden in that gloom.

NO WALKS IN THE FEN

I walked many a field unsure where I would dwell,
Trailing my garments across the coastal shore,
I pass by that misty fen, dark, with ghosts, they tell,
Land with reeds and flowers blooming as many before;

While in that fen, ground's heavy with dew,
I sought that sword to fight those unwilling ghosts,
That place 'twas once verdure while I still grew,
The sword I still seek, to be brave at most;

Once found, I will defeat those unwilling demons, fraught,
And bind all that should be hushed now,
While I see life's dreams and the reasons it's all brought,
And the awe that passes as I wonder how;

I have the spirit to stand forth against them,
Those dark spirits, earth's un-honored things,
I will win that fight to gain that place in the fen,
My ancient place, where I'll wait to see what life brings.

BLUE SKIES

Spring, with its promise of warmth and goodness,
While I am in this odd land, foreign they say,
Shadows flee across this barren land, filled with sadness,
From the farms and the dells, in this early day of May;

Come's faint drawn out sounds, more dead than a bell,
Of some far-off cattle, the echoes unclear,
On those hills where the wind effaces all signs, wherever they fell,
In that mournful waste, to my unsure ear;

Spring is a temple, where, from living pillars, life erupts,
In that shadowy and profound unity, it grows,
As confused words are sometimes, allowed, a flux,
That field, rich, glorious and forbidden, vibrant wherever it shows;

The lake, in light's, and night's, sublime sleep,
While skies rich blue hides, in springs green,
And the mountains listened, to flurries that sweep,
While there 're mysteries that can only by human be seen;

As above my head that indigo sky is silent,
That makes you wish to escape,
I climb those mountains, flowing, but no trace I can descry,
Over sand and bare stone, and sea's stony cold green cape;

I wait for a fragment of music's unnerving beat,
Resembling a human touch unbeknown and thus,
That music of the sea under the blue skies heat,
Whose hand soothes me to slumbers when solace befall' us;

BEAUTY MAYBE

'Where does it come from,' you ask, 'this strange sadness,
That climbs, like the sea, over black, bare stone?'
When our heart has once reaped the harvest,
Life is often evil. That's known;

As the simplest of miseries, and nothing mysterious,
And seen by everyone, in our ecstasy,
Stop searching, you, that one, so curious!
And, your voice is sweet, there's beauty in complexity!

But no, be quiet, you ever ravishing soul!
Lips of childish laughter! Often more than the whole of life,
Death will take us, with subtle lies, uttered without our control,
Let me, my heart then, be drunk on those subtle lies;

I plunge, in a beautiful dream, into your eyes,
And, forever sleep, in your eyelids' shade,
In that shade I see the vanished years,
Dressed in robes outworn, disappearing beyond heaven's rim;

Those delightful eyes, that burn with those mystic rays,
Like candles frail and so pale and white,
But I cannot quench their still, fantastic light they display,
Those candles that burn for the coming morning's light.

ETERNAL DAWN

In calmness, obscurity descends,
Bringing peace to me, and worry to another,
Restless it is, as the moon's indolent dream ends,
A caressing hand, distraught and light, behind that downy cover;

As I watch the white visions of past, that have flown,
Risen like blossoms to the azure sky above,
I'm wrapped in that languor deep, but I should roam!
While Moon breathes a long and swooning sigh, as a brooding
dove;

Alas, clouds like a silken avalanche of soft down, decent upon us,
While dawn came, still hiding the day,
A metamorphosis of beauty, black and rose, still wan,
Sun rises, 'this not fair, I cried, but she's there now, without delay;

Soon she is all one as flower divine, too charming for me to ignore,
As she whispered: "I know of thee",
Like woman's tooth and talons; ah, no more!
With flame-like eyes, that have oft flayed me;

I cannot still that solar fire, my ancient foe,
Tell me, enchantress, who illume that leaden sky,
Am I one of the martyred pilgrims, whispering low?
Or a broken warrior who despairs, as swift hoofs hurry past;

For me I still dream and mourn for that soft moon's light,
Which expands and sinks towards the morn chasm drawn,
But that cherished goddess, so pure and white,
Ever victorious, in that early light of dawn.

SEASCAPE

I see those hills where happiness rest and roams,
Shown in the sun's monotonous fire of delight,
A land where men walk upright and maids haven't yet grown,
That place of remorse, mighty sobs and weary spite;

Light that floats to my soul and my senses throng,
I'm led by that perfume to that land of ease,
A land and ports where many a boat belong,
I await the terror of the fearful breeze;

Masts bend with the burden of the wind-blown thrills,
Sails wearied of the wandering seas, foamy wild,
Am I an exile of this land of sun and forested rills?
I cannot sing of the soul and sense reviled;

Am I one traversing this symbolic sea?
And look on these waters with familiar glee.

DARK MOON

Lingering echo's surround me from afar,
As I see those white painted walls,
Music colorful as brocaded vests, and sounds bizarre,
In that white cave where I seek the love I recall;

We are gathered for that mischief together,
As we see and touch that silent black moon,
While it sheds its dark colored veil of feathers,
We're dark shadows in a park's cold lagoon;

By the sound of angels with evil eyes,
And the falling shadows of the night,
We seek that fire, behind the dark skies,
Kindled by moon's dark and lonely plight,

While during that ambiguous autumn's evening,
We'll seek those dreams without ever believing.

MEMORIES

Twilight grows and memories 'll fade,
Burning hope shrinks and becomes unmade;

Fiery horizons appear and fade with Sun's reason,
It'll fight that mysterious partition of day's treason;

Light flows as in flower's profusion,
With heavy perfumes as a bright warm poison;

We shall have silence, but not repose,
Refreshed, from that bath of darkness, from where we arose;

While a red moon sinks on the misted horizon afar,
Meadows 're filled with dancing fogs their forms bizarre;

Lilies once shuttered are now alive, drowning my senses,
Plane trees stretch far away, calm as in suspense;

Drowning my soul and reasons and their slowly dying cascades,
While twilight grows and memories fade.

REFLECTIONS

While the Sun cast her monotonous glare,
And the yellowing grove shivers in that wind, without care;
We walk that dream, thinking of those aspen's eternal age,
While an olden Sun cast its last rays through that foliage's stage;

Its melancholy not flowing yet, but summer will wane,
And time of chills, gold, onyx and umber, will arrive and remain;
When that Sun will sing in a minor key,
Not penetrating those dark shadows, we do see;

While the chilly wind wrinkles the creek,
Devoid of kindness and charm we still seek;
Gone are those mystical singing birds in summer's breeze,
No more romances without words under meadow's and green
trees;

We must face those chilly words and closed books,
Gone is the radiance in my mind for which she so longingly looks;
But while the sky is copper and devoid of light,
Those trees, in that dream of reflections, are hidden in the
darkness of night;

GREEN

Damp sun in the gray disturbed skies of mysterious charm,
　　　With a treacherous eye that shines through cloud's tears,
but with order and beauty, full of abundant voluptuous calmness,
　　　Verdant greens, and soft moist fens filled with poetry
　　　and virtue;

Alas, if asked, keep me from sin and error grave,
　　　The holy brothers will pass by, like angels wise,
while my soul tries to encompass that landscape of fantasy,
　　　A landscape, hidden beneath a fanciful disguise;

Singing in minor mode of life's beauty 't once was,
　　　And songs mingle with the wan light of the nightly moon,
songs by birds softly dreaming in the trees,
　　　As the night begins to rise;

From the black oaks, in the flickering light,
　　　Comes the nightingale's soft call,
veiled eyes, hidden and dark with mystery
　　　The nuance of green color is absolute;

It will let you dream of cloudy skies and wit forever,
　　　While dawn's wind carries the scent of smoke and seas
　　　alive.

MORNING TIME

Far away from that pale moon and that soft green vale, I so adorn,
    Suns 's silent, looking on through the cloudless sky,
Past that early morn, but still in hiding, as if she's just born,
    Still, she's there, and not a stir of air has gone awry;

Along the brooks margin-sand, water flows listless and calm,
    Reeds standing tall in that dark sodden ground,
Their cold fingers rise in that clear sky without much aplomb,
    But there's much life on this summer's day, that's now
    still unbound;

The feathered grass of vales green and forests with boughs
we know,
    Are hiding forest's live, like crumbled donjons, broken
    and lie still,
Trees standing in abandoned rows awaiting the lighting show,
    Freebooter sparrows come on daring wings and voices
    high and shrill;

Sun's subtly scaling that azure sky, it's elemental power for
us to see,
    Her once slumbering eyes now bright as morning dawns,
This beauty has seized day's splendor with glee,
    As she fights with sword and hand 'against night's
    darkness pawns;

Now that morning's mist is torn asunder by light's streaks,
    And castle's towers are gleaming in her rays,
We see the glory and sun's joy she daily seeks,
    While we hear those larks' song's, pure and glittering
    on the sunny day.

DAYLIGHT

Flowers perfume pure and clear, as day has won,
A slow murmur of the morn's triumphant golden sun,
The kiss of beauty granted with coyness 's gone,
While night's melodies die, thus a mystic farewell, as each
hour is done;

Day's light, as darksome fades will soon shine anew,
While solemn harmonies do attune the string of morning's dew,
And music is showering from this renewed morn's light,
Like the chant of distant choirs, at this new day's sigh;

Now that night has left that barren plain,
And its shadows fall to Sun's daily gain,
I dwell in that rich and radiant array,
That encircle me with its warm and glistening display;

But that glimmer of the night, where are meadows still green,
And the scent of the Arabian vale, soothing as a late rose,
The clouds hide that golden vessel of power and delight,
Flowers fade and verdure glades will decay and blight;

Come will the autumn winds, with their powerful sweep,
Lulling streams and woodlands in their annual chilly sleep,
Nights clouds have those darkest rims,
As days were orange and bright, but now turn gray and dim;

Were the horizon's edge is bound by that brazen golden
rounded ring,
Merging waters and sky in that mutual azure, hiding everything.

FREEDOM

Freedom like the air, it's a spirit of which we dream,
While a warriors dance during the somber night,
Maidens, so young and fair, lights that gleam,
Dance, swifter and lighter as is their right;

Virgins, with skin so white and full of grace,
The laughter, as music following the stave,
While notes are hunting for their rightful place,
In that limpid bay without a single wave;

The cold sea of the north, hides the once smiling land,
Waves roll, with that golden glow, as the tempest blows;
Music is hidden behind those waters foamy hand,
In that calm bay, from where those captive winds rose;

Those dancing warriors swarm as vultures in wheeling flight,
As the chilly northern sea has decreed;
Are they entangled in that shroud of gloom and fright?
As they hold captive those maidens of the air, their freedom
forever denied;

But the sound of echo's is dull and low to vibrate,
As the foamy waves reveals in the rolling liquid,
They are in some hovering state, that we cannot liberate,
That sunbeam shines and dance over the waves colored hides
it depicted.

DAYLIGHT

That seed, that the wind pushed, 'twas still in its husk,
Fresh after morn's balmy kiss, when dewdrops cool,
While Aurora sets out in the roseate feast of dawn,
And Luna sinks, after those far ebony rocks, as a ghoul.

Bramble's thorns bristle like the flinty rocks, so sharp,
As I prowl in that ruddy fog, that's descending,
While in that somber fen I hear that hidden harp,
The kiss of the last night's darkness now ending;

Soon morn's first sunbeam is piercing early dawn, it's still scant,
And the joyous lark, will mount heaven's blush,
On pinions of the air it will fly, singing its never-ending chant,
Past the mountain ravine, and the grove's dreamy hush;

Trembling on that wing, in day's early light,
Bend and frail as a flower 't was in summer's heat,
Morning glances awakening, after the dark voices of the night,
And the sound that grows, is of the nature's greet;

Through the world, schemes of yesterday will commence,
All takes up their story, while children resume their play,
Murmuring and singing, the news is stirred thence,
All of them will hear the story, of that newly born day.

DARK MORNINGS

Through fields and dark glens, I wander,
Climbing those heavenly hills, I've seen there yonder,
Seeking those days, I did squander,
Like dead leaf's that create patterns so bizarre,
Save those that the trees are keeping;

In sun's gracious light and gentle mist, I float,
While flowers of the witch-hazel are still sleeping,
While the airy music plays the notes I wrote,
But my heart is still aching while I seek;

Yet, far off in dim memory is the mystique,
Of those dead leaf's that lie there huddled and bleak,
They I saw my future, for me to fulfil, so to speak,
Memory, oh memory, what do you want of me;

Like a full flight of birds, a dark complexity descends,
As the dew upon me is still un-dried, and wouldn't flee,
The chill' morning wind never ends;
While the sun's monotonous wan glow, slowly extends;

Full of silence and darkness, is the azure sky,
However, melancholy isn't flowing yet,
Rising in pale solemnity, during that night of July,
I left, my soul quivering as if it was ambushed, without
regret.

THOSE DAYS

Dozing in the depths of dismal apathy,
While sun's pierce that hoary oak's canopy,
A new day approaches, with those skies deep blue,
I hide many of my thoughts, that I did accrue.
  In that boudoir, filled with my fantasy,

I breathe the fragrance of those flowers white,
As those whining church-bells ring on,
But the clouds reach out to me,
To shade my desires, in which the soul takes flight,
  While it circles round and round.

As my human mind is set ablaze,
By those thoughts in my soul,
That contains strength and imagination,
But, in my hand I hold the sword,
  To cut away those deadly offering and evil thoughts.

Alas when both of my eyes are closed,
I see those savory fruits of hope,
As your eyes shine with surprising candor,
And I breath in the fragrance of your gilded heart,
  Blazing like white summers sun that's never ending.

A DARK DAY

A flock of birds, dark and brooding,
As memories complex and deep.
Like foliage where light's beams are protruding,
While the sky 's covered with its layer of foggy sleep;

My soul's filled with ennui and fright,
As a dark day, sadder than those dark nights,
Then bells speak out with sudden delight,
And lance the sky with dreams of color and light;

Even the moon with its sallow golden charm,
Wants color before winter's monochrome time,
I dream of flowers in that rural labyrinth of farms,
No matter what storms the paths they may begrime;

I will plunge ever more deeply into autumn's time,
While I wander through my faery palaces of light,
Where hope is but a shadow of summer's prime,
As I wait for spring within, warm with imagination in spite.

FAIR WOMAN

She is indolent and dreamy, as that harvest moon,
A fair woman sitting, resting, during that afternoon,

> Careless her hands lie, gentle and light, beauty as I recall,
> The contour of her breast an avalanche, as if a silken fall,

She breathes, a deep swooning sigh,
With breasts that rise like blossoms in the azure skies,

> And at times, when wrapped in her languor so deep,
> I take in my hand, her tears while she's asleep,

And hide it from the Sun, deep into my heart,
I watch her hair, down in her neck the waves that part,

> And dream upon that sea of amber waves,
> Filled with billowing sails that sing, following the staves,

In this amber ocean where the other ones are hides,
While my subtle spirit will know, the flow of the tides,

> And I sow the stars with gold, that light their white fire,
> So when awake she will hear of my desire.

SUMMER'S BITTER END

Those languorous lands, filled with those aromatic forests wild,
With fertile idleness and fragrant leisure so mild,
    Memories of it's pure and firm measure,
    Where I long, for that azure and bright pleasure;

The heat of the southern climates, as it comes,
There now, but sun's echoes are muted as her execution looms,
    Alas, summer will end and we plunge into those cooling
    shadows,
    While the last vessels glide under her dying golden arrows;

Once it was my oasis and the palette to whence, I did aspire,
When summer was fully undressed for me to admire,
    It is now that ruins, where the Autumn's jackals 'll rest,
    Now there, we seek that dark fruits of summers dying quest,

While I drink her golden crop with pleasure and glee,
We sing that slumberous refrain of being free once again;
    Through the sweeping morning's veil,
    The gusts of autumn's wind will blow their cooling tale,

And during that fierce assault on summer's crumbling bastion,
    We must prepare against the gathering storms, and their
    expansion.

TOMORROW

Tomorrow, at sunrise,
When that glossy golden orb arises from her slumber;

My incomplete dreams sink in that turbulent water,
Will the day arise in its nebulous way?

My dreams engulf me,
But I will trudge on, my eyes sightless and silent;

Saddened that the days will be night for me,
I will not see the golden glow of the morning;

Or the faltering light of dusk,
Those summer's that fly and disappears like swallows.

SHADOWS

They frolic, those angels of the skies, high and cloudy,
While on the roads wind gusts, through meadows, green and
gaudy,
While bells ring their faded tone' wan but with pride,
And shadows push summer's light aside;

Bittersweet is that nightly time when moon hides,
Forgotten and hidden by the dead ones, during those silent
tides,
They died, during those early morn's, dank and dewy,
As my flawed soul is empty and prey to ennui;

But now I see the clear seas, salty as a child's tear,
Golden is the Sun of summer as it lights the paths saints share,
But soon summer will end, and leaf's 'll fall at sun's pass,
And I regret the fading of those young arms of pure grass,

Sun will bury its head, full of pains to winters reign,
And remember, the withered leaf's that will remain,
Into its cloudy skirts it will hide, redolent of its chilly essence,
It's time of mist and past adolescence;

While the prodigious wind is blowing from those depths,
Summer is unable to accept the seasons of violence and chilly
deaths,
Then time arrive of darkness and shadowy disturbances,
And hides that master of celestial furnaces.

MY DREAM

So oft I have this penetrating and weird dream,
Before twilight, when trees spread their branches;
'Mid the languor's of the pine's ancient regime I'm,
    Longing for the arbute tree without those berried patches.

Close your eyes and let those thoughts be,
A feeling of her alone, she 'll knows how to dispel,
Let's go with that gentle cooling winds and be free;
    Gone are summer's sultry afternoons we knew so well.

Sun's exiled now, to that chilly prison, her gold'n light's gone;
My dream's slowly crumble, as paper so light,
But I know those dreams of mine, a call to arms at dawn;
    Now with rainbows lights, deep into my heart, I will fight.

But as beauties, dreamers, lean on my arms,
Dur'ng those ambiguous summer's nights;
I dream while I hear those soft words, deceptive but with charm,
    Of tender hearts, devoid of the vows, for which we must
    fight.

All those memories are beating down on me,
As a cloud of birds, on silent wings, full of dark complexity,
I sleep, while fog's dance in the meadows only for me to see,
    Hiding those dreams of past pain and deep intensity.

LASSITUDE

At that small wooden gate stand a woman, eyes' so blue,
Innocence, looks at flowers in that watery day's light that was due,
In that yellowing wood hidden, from the northern winds, and the
now barren fields,
I hear drowsy tinkling of the incense-breathing morn' as coolness
yields;

Larks twitter on the shed's old crumbling roof,
That woman rests within those flowers, airy and aloof,
Amidst that glimmering landscape that's now in sight,
I wonder what will she think of me, at last harvest' night?

Will I be allowed to wander near her secret bower,
Or must I hide in unfathomed caves where ocean's cower;
Now while the sun descends in the west, birds are silent in their nest,
A flower was offered to her, that counted the steps of the suns quest;

While I awaited her reply, with confusion and without wisdom, As
beauty is concealed by veils of my shadowy vision,
I'm not thinking, but dreaming of love that tire's, during moon' light,
And not the one that caresses leaf's he in the hedgerows crest, despite;

Now that the wheat is gold and the rye is still blond,
I wave farewell to the swallows, that return to climes beyond;
And wait for that woman, the wise, prudent and calm enemy,
In deep shadows wounding, plundering my spoils of distant serenity;

Not without expression of regret, I confirm my crimes, as is my duty,
A woman isn't to be relinquished, while soul aches with ennui
and ignore her beauty.

INNOCENCE

Those seashells are encrusted with sand,
　　On that beach where I seek her soft and tanned hand;

I burn while you are aflame with mocking caress,
　　It has its own peculiarity, never less...

Within the summer's lattice and sun's malice,
　　We tenderly hide our hunger, that had filled us;

As the sea rises with languidly,
　　Her eyes give me promise and validity;

As I dream of romances without guards,
　　Mystical birds fight, over my life shards;

It's innocence that's troubling the horizon,
　　And also, without any logical reason;

There are those tones and many of those odd scents,
　　Hiding life cadences and what it presents;

While love has sated of all those things,
　　It hides the ache and hunger the heart brings.

SONG

During those days in September, gray and chill,
There she was, light, ironic and strong of will;

> I admit, this is the one I admire, without fear or frills,
> She's filled with artless wit and endless trills;

Am I the player of serenades, with many a verse that's tender,
Songs of elegance and joyful surrender?

> I whirl in ecstasy among the wind's gust's, frigid and raw,
> One gilded after another, as I write this verse in awe;

A verse of human grace and amour,
While leaf's fall and we raconteur;

> All with a lofty charm and conquering smile,
> I see and I hear all the joyous retorts, while being guile;

Words born by the swan's pure calm,
Pearly aspects of white and rose, a soothing balm.

NATURE'S SONNET

Time is known, like a picture untainted,
Seeing nature and its season of despair,
Like a woman's heart, not yet acquainted,
    Oft true it is, she'll knows, but it isn't fair;

Gilded is her form as the flower blooms,
Nature's face 's unchanging, I assume,
Like that odd twilight when flowers do groom,
    I have faced her phoenix, oft brooked;

In this world with all her fading sweetness,
I draw those lines with my pen of past,
Lines of my life full and completeness,
    Beauty is surly natures chosen path;

Alas, I flee during nature's time and curse diverse;
    And my love is locked into my verse.

SADNESS

My body that frame, which hold my mind,
My hands that create it painters colored art;
    Will I find a true image that's behind?
    When I gaze thought the window of your heart;

I see the painted beauty in this verse,
As in those young Spring's mornings I have seen;
    And seen that golden face of Sun's traverse,
    While ugly clouds rack that visage, once so clear;

I weep as rain streams against the window's glass,
And sing to that infinite screen of stars;
    Yes, I know there are those eyes, mostly sad ones,
    In my life, as it slowly tars;

I see the folly and an icy heart,
    While the waters sing the last broken part.

BATTLE

Those slopes where angels dance on pastures green,
A place of woe, fill'd with peril, and so oft'n seen,
As field of fire appear round that hilltop high,
There is no need for words, lies or any sinuous illusions thereby;

Engulfed in a library of facts, the honesty of silence wakens me,
Now we've in that mass of clotted rage, we're unwilling to see,
Symbols of madness evaporating after meaningless dreams,
Reason disappears, like footsteps that fade in rivers and
flowing streams;

A desert created for me alone, encircled by a horizon of
tyrannical light,
Light of throbbing sunlight with destroying energy, I will fight,
A labyrinth of mysteries without explanations, an alien dawn,
Now that summer is dwindled and flowers that no longer
spawn;

Across land's tiers the silence rises, a nursery of thing to come,
I feel nature's pulse, fluttering, wondering what I will become,
All my dreams have gone at last,
A new horizon shows, hiding all that is past;

They're good and so beautiful, those summers I've seen,
And of what did remain of my dream.

THE ASTRAL FOREST'S

We humans have nothing that's ours or own,
It truly doesn't matter and does not hurt or is shown,
    We're devoted to what we think we know and avert,
    But those thoughts, recoil us at times we're inert;

Trees whose leaf's flame across the empty sky,
Fragments of time float while memories cry,
    During times when nature has no reply,
    I have memories that I cannot deny;

As I wander, with my head in those clouds,
Stars shine, like silent crowds;
    They float along that coastal sea,
    Following those never-ending waves with a silent glee;

When I lie in bed, hearing that oft played etude;
And that bliss of solitude and pensive moods prelude,
    My heart fills with pleasure seeing the color of the sky,
    I oft devour,
    With the people and the golden times, they must succor;

Now I gaze upon those forests, but with little thought,
    Of the wealth of color that nature has me bought;

DREAMTIME

As I walk on that path, I'm traveling beneath that early sky,
Sowing rhymes as I go, follow a way I cannot deny,
My coat loose and ragged, unsuited for season's time,
As stars lighting the way to that hollow, so sublime;

I stretch out on that pale grass, bathed by that dimming light,
During that nocturnal rest, with moon's shafts pale and white,
Cradled by nature serene darkness and sulphureous dreams,
Catching flashes of the long grasses stems that gleams;

I'll see those memories beaten, ready to drown,
As it did during those last evenings of renown,
Forced into that lake of never-ending regret,
Below that rising of moon I can't forget;

And below that sad splendor of the soaring moon,
Filled with silence and lights, amid that azure lagoon,
A night, melancholic, heavy with that late summer's dew,
Now I'm sure of nothing, of all that's unknown and untrue;

But now in that dreamy and distant land,
    I acquire things, I don't even want.

PASSING SHADOWS

As the shadows pass,
Spectral forms are invoked an mass,
Words 're spoken, but scarely heard,
Each, of itself, ideas ancient but absurd;

On that deserted frozen glass they d'chasse,
High hopes it's under the indigo sky they'll pass,
Rational souls bereft of reason,
As the steersman guides them without treason;

Now that the pale unkept barbarians roam,
As north winds sweep away wave's crested foam,
I sadly contemplate the immense frigid sea,
It's a story of excess love and bitter desire to me;

I will reach the old magic inn's corners deep,
Then awake from the fevers, like a bird on rocks hight and steep,
Where the saline waters will fill me with remorse,
And I hear the night-bird's passing course;

I am afloat in that cold dawns breeze,
Trying to make rhymes to please,
But it's a hollow ring, without that elusive advisor,
Lines are filled with new skies and lovers to seize.

VENGEANCE

Days filled with scents of roses, languidly,
Wafting, the passing in the summer's breeze,
Air fill'd with its own flagrance blend;
With tall branches surrounded,
And the russet rippling grass,
     Like waves flow'ng at your feet;

On this solemn evening,
When black oaks fall;
And the nightingale sings
It's song of despair;
Time's passed,
     And sunlight will return;

Alas, ancient history,
Shadowy wars of humans,
Past tyrants of whom we recoil;
And memories of dark, evil castles,
But mercy is brave, braver than vengeance,
     That we recognise and remember;

Every memory, fantasy and longing is full of ferocity,
It engulfs us in a library of desires,
Humans are eager to strive for the fruit of the nature,
Trembling, swollen and yielding oft, is it's flesh,
There we see the shadows within;
     Hiding the timeless brilliance of nature;

After this, all those scents,
     Are soon forgotten.

HIDDEN SUMMER

I looked on, and ponder'd for so long,
As winds flows down leaf's edges, odd and wrong,
Seeing the forest edge, that was near,
Waiting for rain's erupting drops, with fear;

Watery drops, a chorus 'f hissing serpents,
Courtiers, waiting for intrigues,
Teeming of surreptitious purposes and currents,
While thorny secrets are hidden, without deterrents;

In the catacombs of my mind,
Ghosts of past injuries, hide without origin,
A pool of cosmic terror, that cannot be defined,
And are waiting for the final genesis within;

In that sky of copper, devoid of strong light,
Is a dream that is no longer lives, dur'ng the night,
The moon has lived and died,
And all those unborn fulfilments, I cannot provide;

Events so distant, they are no longer distant,
They'r hiding beyond the horizon, that're not consistent,
Summer is now dwindling away,
A Summers that once drove my heart, it's had it's day;

A dream that is no longer there,
Summer's gone, hiding, unknown as to where,
As I looked on, and ponder'd for so long.

SILENCE

With the memory of the twilight glow,
There are the gifts we'll bring, we know;

Then loves tied to its ivory home,
Among the cypress trees where oft we did roam;

With the memory of that twilight glow,
Like a mysterious partition of the night that grows;

When once, there were flowers in profusion,
Now there nothing's nearer than a shadowy fusion;

A time when precision is wedded with imprecision,
With moonlight show'ng that nightly disorderly vision;

With the memory of the twilight glow,
Showing new skies and love we owe;

Let this be my finest adventure,
Floating on the coming dawn of future;

With the memory of the twilight glows,
And burning hope in lights that's aglow;

But I burned the bridges,
And build walls with no doors or brick ridges;

And where silence says the things,
We all struggle to say.

FUTURE

A day of voiceless trees, lawns bare and brown,
Thunder is there, hiding the force she wields,
    As water sinks in virgin sands, and weeds mourn,
    In that silent forest and the gone barren fields;

I hid in that valley, 'twas light as glass,
Where the sun was still proud in mornings ring,
    Catching the tatters of that last mown grass,
    It's that morn' scent, 't makes my nostrils sting;

Now, nature is deflowered and silent,
Along the yellowed rivers edge I 'll walk,
    Seeing the dry fields of France, defiant,
    With its wayward ditch's and no green stalks;

It's where I'll sleep again as yesteryear,
    As autumn's air calls, and I shelter near.

VALUE

In this life and time,
We think we've seen 't all,
And we wander those paths sublime,
Cherish only the good we'll recall;

  During that fleeting day,
  There're events we don't see.
  We caress life, and its decay,
  Our unknow fate, with glee;

Love oft is true in our mind,
As is the beat within our heart,
But, shadows are blind,
fill'd with hate, which tears our soul apart;

  Emotion paint that picture,
  As we hurtle toward th' future, we've painted.
  That will not last, and isn't richer,
  As the canvas we've already acquainted;

We've painted greens of joy,
Fresh grass beyond compares,
But then comes the age, we're just that "old boy",
Like chrome, that begins to rust and wear;

  The final touches we've created with care,
  And realize the destination is the gallery above,
  But do not let the mind wander too far,
  It's precious to a few, those patterns of love;

On the grass, where days expires
With the first salutes of spectators,
The first twilight has formed, as it retires,
While the doe slips by, as if she is a caretaker;

> Gone are the deities of that morn's dew,
> And the fragrance of sprigs of heath'r,
> Now stars appear as ripe fruit wherever they grew,
> But we and they'll go by, since all must finally pass.

AMOUR

A gentle wind, wrinkle the calm fen's surface,
With reeds so slender, bending lightly,
In the soft breeze like a wing-like tremor.
Shade of summer's leaf's, tremble in the light;

Tender hearts devoid of vows,
As lovers flirt, a hand imperceptibly enlist,
And the promise her eyes gave,
During the passing of summer's breeze;

Alas, open your soul to hear that sound,
Dream, of that fen, azure and silent,
From dawn to evening's sinking sun,
As we chase, bird's last fleeting shadows;

Nightly though, shows the knight eyes,
Pay respect to them, dark and hidden,
While, our hearts beat fiercely,
And we dream of love and liberty.

DAWN

Calmness at summer's dawn,
Of silence profound and senses' ecstasy,
When seeing that fleeing fawn,
And wonder'ng about life' complexity;

I am afraid our life's 're entwined,
As last summer seized our soul,
The silhouette of willow' wet and lined,
There where the winds weep and roll;

As sunflower's emerge from their night's mourning,
Bursting of golden glow, flowers of fantasy,
On that golden carpet is the warning,
When tender balm's falls from heaven's canopy;

As the nightingale sing's,
The future will prove sombre,
We don't know what our slumbering hearts will bring,
At that exquisite hour, when skies are ombre;

Love is full and clear,
Let this silence be without sound,
But, let them all hear,
The voice of despair, when no life is found.

ARTISTS

Painting with many a frail tint to mix,
Create those azure colors that swish,
Flipping tails as if a fish,
Creatures of the sea and it cannot fix;

The creator will pass,
Yet poetry will reign,
And its beauty does remain,
Unblemished as hammer'd brass;

A sculptor reject clay,
Too smooth, in its mind,
There're lines he cannot find,
His thoughts float far away;

Stone and ink that will endure,
Carved with chisel out of that rock,
To be framed in gold without talk or shock,
Finding the beauty blooming to be sure;

An artist studio, is filled but set apart,
Filled with cold pallid light, wan, but full of swirling strokes,
Beauty dazzled me, that the light invokes,
Creating a fragment that's human art;

Alas, with a delicate hand that follows,
He works, that agate's vein,
Something I couldn't attain,
Beauty blooms within the form of that hollow.

DREAMER

During that gold'n summer's day, so clear and bright to play,
I ramb'ling through fields I knew, trampling early dew,
Yes, a dreamer I am, while underfoot the coolness grew;
I dream of that flowery day, a rural labyrinth of light, they say;

A world of sunlight, when birds singing in that grove,
With new things, we might discover on lover's porche;
Then nightly I sleep up high, with the starry course,
And I see mountains of eternal immensity, that I'll behove;

Memories of that morn's soft twilight glow,
With hope that burns and grows without reason,
Fill'd with heady perfumes and that warm poison,
Skies that are delightfully soft and devoid of vows;

At day's ends the red moon rises from a misted horizon,
Among the brush fireflies call with that silent light,
Tall and serried the elms stretch along paths right,
Where owls fly their soundless flight, seen by no one;

But now, with night's mystery drawn;
And time of infused teas and hidden illusions,
We feel the sweet feelings of evening's conclusions,
And dream together, when sunlight spawn's in early dawn.

POETRY

The evening time has come,
With its scent, sounds and gentle fume,
The sky lofty altar's color'd red, but still bright in even'ngs gloom,
Where the drowning sun, her blood st'll glowing, will succumb;

Will the rising moon's dreams, and fall in that deep'r languidness,
She rises, as a beauty within that satiny cocoon,
But yield'ng to that unending daily swoon,
On the nightly altar, where flowers ar' strewn in expansiveness;

Each flower sifting its perfume with tentative caress,
Like those dwindling echoes returning from far and forth,
Perfumes sweet as a lute's chords,
Ecstasies of sense, and soul's excess;

Poets makes their appearance in this dull world,
A world, filled with hate, but avenging treachery,
But the wild bird's sing of innocent gaiety,
While poets' ride those storms, with wings unfurled;

I cast a sensuous balm, unburdened and unbound,
By his sweet repose, with words and veils of shadows, I've wrought,
Night's yellow moon hover's overhead, in darkness where
time's now caught,
While I wait, slowly that skein of time is unwound.

ART OF LIFE

Tired I was, it touched m' consciousness,
On that wood'n floor is total bareness,
    Amid my paints 'nd brushes, old and well worn,
    But no filth, or sour'd air, is 'n this dell, I adorn;

No withered wood touch'd the light of my soul,
My mind 's clear, without strain or hidd'n goal,
    Now among the fens 'nd mountains there, I must lay,
    Where dawn is smiling, and dew is nearby;

Seeing those roses pale, their kiss of buds, before they blaze,
Summer's com'ng, when they bloom and care,
    Time to send dreamy lovers 'n their secret ways,
    Away from my abode, work and places, we did share;

I dream 'f butterflies flying out wide,
Who seek through clouds 'nd lights bright, souls to love,
    But then leave the lady mistress in despair,
    To flit to flowers, being sweeter and more dear;

With a fond heart, within my billet I'm bound,
with the soft silk paper upon which my brush glides,
    fill'd with messages of love, that mortals write,
    and dreams of summer's delight;

I love those evenings, trees leafage close, still sheer,
Alas, now I seek the lost companions of our days,
My work is't here, it's the spirit of another sphere,

    There where countless sunbeams splinter in golden arrays;
    Beneath the solemn beauty with that azure mystery infinite.

THAT GOLDEN SAND

In that sun and golden sands, is my dreamy lair;
Where fluid, in that languid saline bath, her hair flows
You're my pride, of shadows' a breath of fire,
As through those blue summer's nights, I repose;

Away from cafés and their dazzling gleams,
I dream while under shadow's wings,
Where I ran off dressed in m' ragged seams,
To that sweet hollow where that river sings;

I dreamed of amorous groves and luminous swells,
Flowers and starry nights, fill'd with wheaty country smells,
As that river let me float down, a stream that doesn't falter,
Into the furious breakers of the cold north'rn saline waters;

Now I see the low sun, filled with that mystic'l terror, she wield'
But my pride, it stands' firm in that green field,
Amidst the insensibility of rocks and the azure sky,
As was certain of my dream, desired in my eye.

SMILING

Here on that olden floor,
Footworn 'nd hollow now, 't was,
Into that beaten straw wall,
A former door, wher' dead feet once pass'd;

Smiling into that glowing fire, she sat,
While hoar frost was spectre-gray,
Winter's last dregs, made desolate;
Land's sharp features outlined as a corpse;

Childlike I danced in that dream,
On music' of broken lyres strings;
Emblazoned on that very day,
But now day's eye's 're weakening;

But I couldn't look away,
From that last glowing gleam,
Of the woman's blooming life,
While I laugh and sit alone;

When everything pass's and vanishes,
Everything 'll leave no trace,
But oft you see it 'n a footstep,
What you couldn't see in a face.

SUMMERS DREAM

That end the summer I'll weep and utter this lament,
As I did esteem myself and th' times 'll boast,
People wonder, and some but not most, Poetry has a purity,
All know, I think, surely,
As a soul's fill'd the host, quite demurely,
But now, as natur's spittle, grinds and crushes,
And we discover summer's eve, between the rushes;

That heavy, blank, despotic Summer, world-weary,
With memories of that twilight light glowing,
Shaking in that far horizon dim and eerie,
A mysterious apparition of hope, growing,
With flowers, multicoloured showing,
Flying round the grove, in circulation,
In sun's warmth as a heady exhalation;

Tell me that's brave at most,
Will that Sun beg for more spending,
What will the season cost,
Did God's miracle remove season' ending,
And make souls feel what he's sending,
In this dream a terrifying vision is present,
Questions never ending, as a disease is doubling it's own rent.

LIFE

Winter's gone, and summer blooms,
Sorrow is replaced by glee as hotness looms,
    All at once I laugh and cry,
    My voice will rise, but is still shy,
The spirit in this mortal abode, being short,
Now no longer are there signs of love fort;

But with my heart being strong and anew,
I will resist those sobs that I always brew,
    As long with my mind I can still encompass,
    Pleasure that still will be sound like rumpus past,
While I smother this rose and hold it to my heart,
I won't shake it, and it will not take us apart;

And thus pushed to newer shores and lands,
Casting my anchors for eternity,
    However void and foreign those sands,
    In those days buried, I saw those sights unknown,
Time will evade me and being let alone,
    Let me savoir those fleeting delights,
    I did postpone, From those many day's, life has shown.

MINDSET

Eyes like dead leaf's, joy that's freely spend,
My spirit has faded, like dream's untrue,
Moon's crescent left light as a poor lament,
Dying ghosts rising like mist that's still due;

Life is draining from the soil, once fertile,
A nursery of new things, as unborn dreams,
A power beyond my unaid'd eyes guile,
It's in those dreams all those things live it seems;

In that place where the foaming sea gently spills,
Those dreams that drives the heart and become's true,
Dreams like music at that window's sill's,
How poignant were the abandon'd hopes we knew;

But, I am becalmed in the still air,
It's summer, when birds gather and care.

SEASCAPES

The sun stood tall in dawn's azure sky,
It's light still rimmed with gold.
Far away clean white sails, leaning, as if gone awry,
I follow her, quieter than the waves, when in she roll'd;

While the seabirds circled aimlessly,
Seaweed drifted by as I tread the surge of the sea,
The last glimpse of her ship's wooden ribs shown shamelessly,
Devoured by turbulent waves, for all to see;

While the sonorous seas beat beneath sun's grieving eye,
Victorious waves rise, burst and shout,
And in the tall skies, where dark storms live and cry,
I am lulled into that damp colorless dawn, where clouds sprout;

Alas, now that the sun fills the thinning skies,
We'll build our rainbows before sun's light dies.

VENUS THE CRUEL ONE

Cruel Venus, you veiled beauty, ill-natured and unworthy,
Your doom's harsh and so malicious.
Why to a fair lady won't you show mercy,
To whom 's so loving, kind and courteous?

Withdraw your opinions and be gracious,
Whom, that never have been able to agree,
It's shows what you are hidden and <u>voracious</u>,
A vengeful sentence w'll be passed soon, we'll see;

Treason will prosper, but what is treason,
For if it cannot prosper, none will dare to call it treason!
Hence, your opinions are veiled, without reason,
Will thou listen to the words of my mourning tongue's reason?

Dur'ng moonless nights we saw your soft light,
While I eye-guess that pleasant vale, where I lay,
But you hide thy beauty and sheen so slight,
Then send forth harsh thunder and light'ng rays that day;

I had put my trust in you, O, Venus, you queen of love,
Are you the false Cupid, a love blind goddess?
A planet full of ire, and dissention that you behove,
So god that shakes my worlds, and isn't honest;

You're sweet at times, but oft, bitter and sour,
Unstable as always, ever variable, your branches rough,
Never an honest one, you try to devour me,
As autumn leaf's that fell, now withered on my vale's bough.

I DREAM MY SUMMER'S DREAMS

Alone in that land, a wolf's den, of darkn'ss and piercing chill,
Getting lonely, and growing old, as I follow wind's will;
I consume by woes, and talk to those dank dripping woods,
Muse of that Sunnier land, loftier than this wolfish hood,

I hide my love of fields in hidd'n dells,
Where dew drops pearl onto the hidden blue bells;
I long for hilly scenes, there where man cannot trod,
I'll see the winds of the ancient lands of God;

Amid that blue skies commotion, I wait for Gods fleeting demands,
As swift clouds flee, stroking shores with their feathery hands,
I see their soft brush, and am lull'd by those crystalline streams of light,
While I dream my summer's dreams and of that Mediterranean delight;

I'll hastened to the sands where I dwelled once,
Where I mingled and was opposed to that forbidden sconce,
As soft music plays, time slides, and moon's lights hides,
Love itself lies dead, like unlit rainbows that lost their glory and lighting pride;

In that soft grass below, I look up at that vaulted sky,
 And reach out to grasp that time, as it is running by.

RÊVES

The trouble is not the graying clouds or the soft rain,
And misty vistas among the rolling hills,
Showing those rocky outcrops;

I seek that long golden beach,
Glorious sand, covered in that soft cloudy moisture,
While I chase for that hidden blemish of Suns light;

Sun within that cloudy sky,
Will I find it before the beach ends,
Love will guide me towards that lonely river;

The river that separates my dreams and hers,
Rain like her skin, soft and tender,
But hidden in those misty clouds;

I dream of those lonely abodes surrounded with turf and weeds,
While I wander along those green grassy banks,
Of unfolding future and hope.

GONE IS SPRING

Gone are the songs of spring,
Clouds gather, obscuring that once blooming day,
Winnowing winds gather those noisy leaf's,
Fallen, now amber and gold,
And gone are the songs of Spring;

Where are all that birds twitter in summers sky,
Beauty's lost, as flowers fade,
But this is not a poem full of hurt,
Or filled with mystery and the essence of God,
But beauty, filling the last days of summer's light;

Coming darkness and chill that 'll decent,
I'll look at the sweet tragedy of year's end,
Shadows of absent memories past,
Seeing that bare landscape in my mind,
Eroded memories of none, but late Sun's light;

Now in that time of mist and rip'ng the vines fruits,
Waiting by that wine-press for the last oozing of juice,
Gone is that nightingale now, singing its Provençal songs,
Faded away into those forests, now dim and grey,
Gone are the songs of Spring;

Now I see that wilted flora and bare country lanes,
Gone is that leaf fringed legend of past years,
Summer, is tired of life, but scared to die,
As an unmasted boat 's loose at the sea,
Gone are the songs of Spring;

Time of tawny dreams is here,
Pale moonlight and mist shrouded horizons,
Golden meadows with swirling evening fog,
And those racing clouds in tall skies blue, but;
Gone are the songs of Spring.

SEDUCTION

Passions, we call love,
Tender and full of fire,
A game, or erotic needs?

I recall when I was in love,
Belgium, that bastion of hidden silence,
A frivolous world of religions;

At nights, of full moon,
I would sing songs without words,
Painful freedom without pleasure;

I assume that mask of the night
Reliving those jarring memories,
Of sleepless nights in cold barren places;

Am I that bird, contemplating,
That test flight in the dark skies,
When has dawn not yet roused me from it's sleep?

Perhaps that soft moon that lit that dream,
Black against the evening sky,
My life is of which I dream of, love that grows free;

But, now that I have left my lyre to youth,
Others will take that joy,
As I have been seduced by love.

AUTUMNS WINDOW

The big forest winds down, to the bank where branches stir,
Filled with elm, laurels and those tall firs,

Set in that soft valley I know so well,
I hear that tone, dulcet and warm, saying days farewell;

The Sun stood firmly in the smooth cerulean sky,
The darkening valley edge still showing, but shy,

Shattering the visage of the day's triumph,
As stars sown cloaks enfolds it, now
that Sun is without alliance;

Nature has stepped down of her timeless bank,
The horizons filled with wisps of past songs as last thank,

Windows of life receding in shadowy nights,
Swept on that tingling tide of time and the dark light;

That ending time, is unkind in closing days guise,
Though wise men know that dark is
right, when light rays die,

Seen in the window where light their frail deeds dance,
With rage against the fading days romance;

I sail against the day's running tide,
Cursing with fierce tears against that unfading divide;

A wild call that I cannot deny or resume,
My life path's cut by winds whetted knifes and blown spume.

WINTER TIME

Early evening gathers, cold as 'n icy fist,
Waves struggle with winter's wild winds,
I've only memories of that sunrise and early mist;
A vague dream of life I lived behind summers blinds;

Images of past days and the shimmer of high noon;
Now the wind hurls itself at cliffs worn smooth and bare,
The once sunlit countryside w'll turn to ice soon,
Then it 'll spreads its silent white carpet fully and without care;

Moon cast her cold light onto dark cloud's bed,
While the fire burns and coughs in my worn grate,
Not there to warm my heart or light the already dead,
But to honor the falling leaf's and vanishing days fate;

Will my future be in those cold antique lands,
And will I suffer that cruel wind,
Squalling and scouring the moving sands,
I walk that old groove, now frozen, trees stoop'd and blind;

The stand where oaks reside calm in half-light,
Casting their deep shadows silently,
Merging as one soul, despite,
That cruel wind gusting violently;

Now winter has arrived, unleashing her fury and cold beauty,
Filling me with subtle poison and that fading hope,
Hope, colder and more piecing than winter's booty,
Spoken by those sapless leaf's with no future scope.

NIGHTLY AIR

Sleep, smooth as a glossy tide,
Eternal problems are resolved,
Simplified and glorified,
Politics 'r gone, pure fantasy, unresolved;

But the tide, that swell of the unknown,
Waiting for its fateful daily pause,
As the myriads of airy sprays that 're blown,
Over earth's face, with all her ancient flaws;

Air swirl like muslin, in sea's spray's,
Give me your hand, and let us rest,
In moon's caress 'nd her soft rays,
With the night's nocturn's still unstressed;

Life's cruel, with no vintage from oth'r shores,
To fire my tired and jaundiced heart,
Limp hands and flickering eyes without shine,
A body strain'ng to grasps those floating air's parts;

Alas, let's not forget to hope, discreetly,
So the heart of each of us stays intent and learn's,
Dur'ng those calm nights, as moon's rays shine sweetly,
While air and nature fight, fierce and taciturn;

While she's prudent and wise, but's 'n enemy,
Never show'ng victory, only steel and distant toils,
Fickle as the winter's air, chilly, yet full of serenity,
That air, contrived, unseen, is't holding my destiny and joys?

SNOW

January 't will appear with wind and sleet,
It's eve's now, with a long dark weariness,
Fire glows, showing summer's crimes with intense fieriness,
And moon's beams light'ng those times unrefined;

Then, morning time, whence the opal gleams start,
Flakes of snow drop like tears, sleep departs,
Gone are those autumn's eves of gold,
Unkind, but 'tis led by that perennial perfume, it behold;

'twas a time profound, life did flow, full of joyfulness,
I drank it's breath, alas, sweet and poisonous,
Autumn's gone, snow, wants to visit us,
To make its magic, and strike me without any fuss;

Soon storms, hoar-frost and ice reign's,
The dead and dark horizons move in the plains,
I brush snowy flakes 'f granite scalps,
As winter's put out as lightning in snow filled alps;

Now the snow has cloaked the plains,
And those boughs and grove's lanes,
Flakes as feathers from sea-gulls wings afar,
Those sequins shining far as stars;

Winter's time, wind moans and snow falls, as 'n fairy show;
I see that interminable landscape, and the glitter of snow,
Earth 's barren, but can it sustain winter's affections?
Snows silent carpets 're hidings earth bleak imperfections,

It has found here a home,
Speed quickly, you steeds of time, no reason to roam,
Across the branches hiding the fleeting snow;
Winter's time, wind moans and snow falls, as 'n fairy show.

MAYBE

Images that blend, is what we behoves,
Senses fill'd with ecstasy, we'll see,
Cathedrals hidden in green groves,
Where trees droop, without glee;

I adore that hidden ocean, and the sting of saline air,
Being free from all the futile endeavors,
Let us yield, you and me,
To nature's balm, calm and sweet;

At the nightingale's soft call,
Our despair avers, and we solemnly accept,
But now our life of silk and pearl rosary, 's gone,
That time was neither a dream nor real life;

I am beaten by the wall of nothingness,
Will I still live in your heart, at least,
Or am I a memory, now absent,
My hopes 're fended off, and doors slammed.

POET'S LAMENT

Listen to that sweetest song that'll pass,
To weep with sole delight,
It's discreet, and ever so light,
Water-drops trembling an mass;

Hatred and envy will go,
What's left, death 'll enshroud it,
Our life is goodness, that we know,
Like lifting birds on a drifting boat's sprit;

I don't choose these words in ease,
Filled with confusion in mind's vision,
When shadowy verse, dear to me, oft it does not agree,
And my mind tries to wed many 'n indecision;

But who'll tell me the magic of my rhymes? I
f I don't look out, where will they go?
Words are 'n adventure, afloat on dawn's gold'n time,
Oft filled with happiness, and sunlight that's aglow;

Now, on the vague crest of that foreign rise,
I'll stretch out my wings, yes heavy with madness,
Imagination firmly enthroned in that hidden guise,
As I write this verse without words or sadness.

YEARS END

Farewell rolling fields 'nd leaf filled groves;
Gone are daydreams, of looking in loved one's eyes,
No more laughs while hiding 'n those grassy coves,
With the sensations of what a soft evening' ending implies;

But as tall lily's, rock in cooling winds,
And the mignonette flowers 're now well past their last flush,
Swallows fly, their annual journey south begins;
While vines 're ripe, their opalescent fruits dark and lush;

I'll see that dark lake with year's rising regret, clear and fast,
And sun's last tremble on that fiery horizon afar,
Showing the pale solemnity, of summer's nights, now past,
Gone is that mysterious hope, of seeing Hesperus, the even'ngs star;

History' dying away, as leaf 's crumple, and drop at wind's cue;
While earth fills her chilling lap with pleasures unknown; Now first
the mist decent, to hide nature's corridor of dew,
While I run without reason it the bleak light still shown;

My spirit, is like my pillar 'f strength, ardently prays for rest;
While my heart 's always full of dreams,
Year has ended, now voluptuous winter' nights 'll rise, calming my quest,
Stinging autumn now gone, an illusion of end of time, so it seems;

Now that year is clear, I compose this solemn verse,
Listen to the calm hymns and watch the birth of verse's I know,
I will not heed the stealthy tread and sinful words will persevere,
As all seasons will pass, and winter 'll approach with his weary snow;

My nocturnal ordeals of memories w'll remain,
And I'll travel without sail or wind behind,
Seeking the bitter knowledge that wanderers gain,
Of the sorrow's still hidden in words that 're are everywhere enshrined.

DO NOT LEAVE ME

Fog, during the night' has come,
Shrouding the town afar,
The spend Sun droops,
On the horizon red and bizarre;
Shadows entering my scaffold,
Filled of searing dreams;

> "Waiting for season's annual funeral teams,
> While day's slowly crumbles and winter gleams"

Vision and time take no prisoners,
So I am told,
As I dream of that golden voyager,
now foolish and old,
And see that dying year's end,
With sorrow and despair;

> "While I draw those figures in the soft sands,
> I wait for those dark days that seasons w'll demands"

I remember the sun's glinting supreme rays;
Shining the length of the pond,
Tracing the shadows that play,
Stirring echo's of summer's golden past,
When teal-duck's calls were amassed;

> "But now hearses roll surely,
> And bells toll with their fury"

Now within the gloomy boughs,
she promised to console me;
I will not repeat the beguiling verse,
I wrote once with glee;
I 'll endure the snowy time, bereft of comfort;

> "While my eyes swam with undropped tears,
> And see day's fall in decay of winter's snares"

SPRING THOUGHTS

Touched by those soft lips and starlit hands,
Bound by that shadowy hour of those ethereal bands;
>Behold, awake, it are dreams, that silent heart's make,
>During the rising of the audacious Sun's gilded gleam!

Hidden are those thoughts in the invisible sea's wrongs,
As birds soar to the sound of mourning violin's songs;
>Music so sweet that the spring day is a framed measure of my soul,
>And is the opening of nature's yearly birth and role;

In fair times, seasons nature's springtime links,
While frosty air is still keen and silent, as Sunrise pinks;
>There is no need for words, engulfed in that world of desires,
>Spring is blooming with honestly and with the silence she requires;
Awake, we will decent from that world beyond,

With words of understanding we will respond;
Spring is coming, unblemished, filled with those beads of water,
>And with the youth, that we hope will be there,
>Dreams 're gone now, future is new;

>We wait for that unborn hope.

NEW LIFE

In the orchards and many a field,
Fireworks sounds and flames they do wield,
    Early snow, at the end of year,
    While logs dropped onto stony yard's sound so near,

Now sun's hidden, in a cold and a dismal place,
Yesterday's summer, 's gone, with no last embrace;
    As I sit alone in that grove, lingering there,
    With memories of times, clear and fair;

But gaiety and pleasure are still abound,
While shadows hide, the mist drenched lakes all around;
    And the mellow fruitfulness under that maturing sun,
    with the glean of apples on mossed trees that has begun;

Dawning of a new year, cold and frigid as the moon is now,
A legend somber and bent to bow,
    In those days, clouds 're filled with doom,
    As light transfigured unseen, in that dark room;

I wait for mornings call, when soft Sunrises will resume,
the flutter of day's pleasures, as the trumpet's blare, and springs
will bloom;
    Outside the rivers of smoke are rising, in dark streams,
    But I remember the kisses in the glade of our dreams,

With that young golden Sun, soft and tender, as she sang,
Life will restart, among the cloudy veils, where the winter will hang;
    A new year filled with sound, fire and barking hounds,
    Let our heart rejoice and love that yearly voice without
    any bounds.

BEAUTY

Beauty, it does visit's us from the sky,
It's infernal and divine and we do not know why,
Our hearts hold that craving, during those dark days,
It moves yonder as if wild ocean's brine, without ways;

Clouds condemned, filled with those promised flakes,
They float slowly and with the sublime infinity it takes,
We walk on with beauty and are sorrow for what falls beside,
That white snow, calm as fair rivers will ever glide;

Snowflakes so tender, as softly they dance to their final doom,
Light, raw and cold, in fractured lines follow flakes final
drifting path,
It call's to mind those chill enshrouded days of recent past,
Tender in turn, dreamy, but still merciless;

A shifting sky, dark, it's beauty mirroring life,
Snow falls on those wayward hills,
Pale glow of moon's light, transfiguring that silent world,
Showing nature's artistry and beauty without any words;

Towards that beauty, full of wintery dreams and
wonders,
Days in which we are captives and are defeated, as in so
many others!

RAINY DAY

In that empire of decadence, that's abound,
With fading light and spider's departing sound,
I'll hear the sobs of autumn's violins, all around,
Laying waste of that already barren ground;

      I drink that wine of foreign shores, not so divine,
      As a melancholic pilgrim, when age declines,
      Searching for those faded land's,
      While soft drops fall, in those river-driven bands;

Memories of Paris it's river fully stretched,
Like a snake, gleaning in the soft rain, enmeshed,
Bouquiniste's hide their printed dreams,
While rain straggles to cover all cheer, in streams;

      Plane trees shed their dripping leaf's,
      While their wet shadows die as if smoky thieves,
      I watch and see them fade,
      In that flutter of autumn's airy crusade;

But I've those memories of freedom, that I have won,
Drunk of the early summer's sun,
Riding those thoughts, and turbulence full,
In the barking and scavenging winds, that autumn pulls;

      In the streets of those magic towns,
      I write words, as bouquets of fading flowers that winter
      downs,
      While music dissolves in the air,
      And my painted images only shimmer in late summer's light
      still there;

Rain covers my world of light,
It'll torment glassy lights and silent those nights,
Creating that muddy labyrinth,
In that thirsty grove full of yearly myths.

DAWN

Sky shut, locked in its own grave, it befell,
And sun's spirit looks for year's coming chime,
Now nature, has sharpened her honed knives well,
And is looking in my heart's granite shell;

It will gouge and destroy all words I create,
Of that imperishable rhyme and magic,
Gripped by natures strong might, I must wait,
In darkness, black as night, oft cold and tragic;

But I write these words, rising without shame,
Nature wakes, it doesn't speak of tombs and dead,
Dawn is not an end of what it became,
It is a birth that'll come soon instead,

> Of vestal days, in old rooms long since gone,
> Nature will show glory and charm at dawn.

THE SUN

It fill's our mind and its nourishes the crops to grow,
With grace's it's does her daily rounds, alas passionless,
We're imprisoned now, in these dogdays of clouds and late snow,
Unseen is that ruby dawn, with promises that could gladden our
dreams;

We think of that perfect blue spiritual sky, in our dreams,
While our lives have moments of touching those celestial strings,
Violins tremble, as hearts 're filled with hope that gleams,
But oft our despotic rulers ruin the life onto which we cling;

Diseases without control engulf us, in a steady tide,
Like a pall of mist it'll enshrouds us, silent and dun,
Sun's wrapped in that dark abyss, to which we must abide,
Thirsted with emotion, my heart oozes rebellion, not seen by any one;

I know the Sun has left these shores,
Celestial clouds racing and are scudding wild,
While as an artist, I doodle those lazy circles that people adore'
And write words that are fades flowers, contemn'd, and oft reviled;

But as an emerging dream, the Sun appears showing that early spring,
Gulley's of tears run down my cheeks, as I think of those new dreams,
Summer's coming, green dells, and the silken sound of bees taking wing,
Now the crazy signs 'll appear, that no one can see or answer;

Let us find that new grass where bud's glisten,
Welcome that splendor of the bashful new dawn,
Saying those soft words, to which no one will listen,
Let me drink the dew of the young grass mellow, and follow that fawn.

SPRING

In the ancient forest I walk, seeking those velvet swards,
Admiring the silvering of birch's barks and plants, still
unprepared,
Life is a constant torrent of musings, with little rewards,
Now I'll ponder in that dark and gloomy verdage;

I see clearly the mingled truth in the leaf laden pines,
Among the shadows is the answer to those mysteries;
Spring will arrive, and young cresses will flow round as winter
will resigns,
I'll see the savage beauty of those young leaf's victories;

A new spring 's born with charm and a conquering smile,
Fill'd with dreams of russet grass and solemn warm evenings,
Time that hearts and souls blend, while we slumber awhile,
Wondering of futures meanings;

Now I dream of shadowy trees along mist drenched rivers,
With wind driven waves and their magic at the horizons edge,
I found my fields with the velvet swards that shiver,
Filled with clover and pale sedge;

Seeing the dew that the dawn wind froze,
In a sky soo blue, and in which Moons golden orb still glows.

RETOUR

In the pale forest of exile, I am not at ease,
I wander among the frost silvered yew-trees,
Dreams of fields with innumerable flowers,
As the afternoon fades, while its sweetness still towers;

> In that alien land, now so forsaken,
> Bruised, summer's future will soon awaken,
> And show's joy of peace without victory,
> As morn's early light beams are filled with mystery;

I was that leaf winding down from the west,
Sleeping on sea's placid breast,
Coursing past where aurora start her roseate waste,
And go that place where fields are bright, with haste;

> Live, admits corns golden tresses that 're entwining,
> And furrows not yet shorn but bare unbinding,
> On that ripening breast I place my head,
> Dreaming of those cherished moments, left unsaid;

In that château and the streets in that magic town up high,
I will dab those rivulets of tears, you will cry,
While I take the road that few men will try,
And feel the delicate elegance of time while we say our
goodbyes.

MEMORIES

Let's go then, just you 'nd me,
Away from tedious hotels where nights we do not see;
Go in the smoke and darkness 'f that December's afternoon,
We'll think of about our fate, too soon;

I will create our life, before it is too late, in those fields perhaps,
Then, amidst withered leaf's, like grimy scraps, we'll collapse;
Thinking of the burned-out ends, in the smoky haze,
Yet, in the mid of this universal time, we dream of summers rays;

Of vividness, and color, as we decent the stairway from the
clouds,
We think of the absent lands, and their forms that darkness
its enshrouds;
Quarrels forgotten, wrongs forgiven, memories fled like smoke,
The sea, infinite and with terrifying simplicity, recalls of what
we spoke;

My desire of nuances, color and your wit,
During those days that quiver, while sunlight graces it;
Now summers days have arrived, beneath cold souls they hid,
But now Sun's soft tender rays caress those fields, now fully lit;

Let us sing and weep to dissolve those past memories,
Let the spread of Sun's beams light up those young treasuries;
And see all the girls, whose honor we might save,
Lives with Sunlight and no treason, lips with no lies, for that
we did crave.

NATURE'S TRUST

The Moon, softly descending from h'r throne of magnificence,
With it's youthful magniloquence;
Reflected in that still and simple ocean of utter silence,
She's in a state of reverie, of total absence;

That Moon, waiting, a dream of delight, during her nearing
eclipse,
A beacon over a world of pain, pale-cold now, are her once
crimson lips;
When mortal hearts weep, and her decent is cried out by many
a sentinel,
She was born in that roseate evening sky, without a cloudy
disguise;

Still we're wrapped 'n that languor deep,
Poets, whose enemy are asleep;
Create their words, with sadness and tearful eyes,
But under that charming Spring sky, they too will rise;

Now, gone are those pleasantries, filled w'th peril,
We welcome nature's tenacious power, to hide Winters chilly
apparel;
The young air is heavy with rumors, vivid and strong,
Summer is approaching with day's bright and long,

Now beyond that new flowers orgy, music chants during
springs glory,

Nature, that cherished enchantress, tempted by colour and
that silent story;
An annual duel of beauty and terror, when artistry is defeated,
And we mortals, admire the time when the colorless chill has
retreated;

Summer is a time of kindness, alas, 't has felt hate,
Hate, that angel of mistrust and pain so great,
We know it, the fear of age, as even summer has to wane,
Reading that horror in a smile, that's nature's annual domain;

When the time approached, stems will 'ncline,
Color evaporate like incense burned on natur's shrine;
Scents wane in vesper's windy turns,
Skies are like a mosaic soft but stern;

Our hearts are like palaces empty and pillag'd,
That last roseate sky turns with chilling speed to bleakness
we imaged;
And like the woman's biting grip has left many a trace,
We hear that frozen melody of nature's trust, we must now
embrace.

MORE DREAMS

In that tangled web of my mind, birds flee in ev'nings crimson
clouds,
That lone fisher, rods aflame, far out at sea,
Nets slack, as wind smite waves, he prays in holy fright,
Ready he stood with parted lips, but calm brow;
While nights Moon hides, not show'ng her tawny mask;

Spume hides those hidden rocks over which rising water flows,
And that rolling ship on which the fisher stood,
Leaping in that chill and churning foam, beat'ng for that rocky
shore,
Seas quench my self-fed flame as Dawn's light flitted in that glade,
Showing wood-nymphs circling in the tangl'd wood;

When day breaks and that moonless night wanes,
I look at the turbid turquoise skies, waiting for Suns early rays,
Past winter's air was keen and cold, chilling natur's glades,
Now young leaf's start their orgy, and fleeing birds do return,

Morning's memory is firm and fateful, seeing beyond that veil,
Sun quivering in a sky pale, showing its gold'n head,
Now children's voices whisper in the vale,
Then as nightly dew rises in the dale, it's filled with play they
cannot curtail;

Now that winter's thrown down it's spear,
We can love and cry without fear.

WHENCE I CAME

Amidst the forest gnarled branches, ring'd doves move without pause,
Swift 'nd silent they flee, never a sound they'd make,
Just as flowing water, fast and quietly th'y crawl,
Opaque and black, yet peaceful, without a break,

Cold wind hurls itself 't bushes black,
Sunlit countryside turns snow to ice,
Waiting for natures fin'l attack,
Standing light illuminating those tender greens, as trees rise;

Now in that dark land's cold ponds,
A place where I lived once but can't answer to,
All 's shut now, that isle of bluebells and roses, 'll not respond,
Alas, our small and tedious world, giv' us little pleasure to accrue;

While in the endless barren fields, the winds provoke,
'll travel, leaving behind morning's dew,
To find a refuge from the bare fields and the sadness they 'll invoke,
In that gully green and that golden light new;

There I will sleep as the mountain-sun foams with light,
And listen to natures music's nervy breath,
Image the sun's shimmer at noon's height,
Image the woods tremble in wind's last bite and h'r death;

Now in those sweet days of happiness beyond words,
With blue skies and short nights instead,
I go among those rough grassy dells, filled with many a birds,
With only the nights to hear what is said.

NEW HOPES

Rose-scented air of those days past,
Flowers and honey bees caress,
When time moves too fast,
Smell of honeysuckle and lilies are the secrets it possess;

Now with the silv'ring of birch's bark,
In the half-lit glades, I create,
Color to paint it's verdure dark,
I ponder of my latest work avoid'ng debate;

When 't night rain swallow's land,
And Venus 's shown only as a starry spark,
I hear that ill fated command,
To bring m' future out of the dark;

I create my pictur's in vain,
In exile, bitter, without a term,
But I accept, nor seek or care to remain,
Art painted to make heart's dance and summer's affirm;

In my path I often stray,
Life whirls with eddying waves,
Forgotten sweeps and wan days,
Awake the butterflies 'd follow the path they waives.

SHADOWY VERSE

That sentimental friend,
The nightly moon, strolling in the sky,
Like a battered light, held aloft,
Showing me the worn edg's of the path I'll walk;
I met her there, sad an' broken in that fading light,
As a twisted branch on that dim path,
Now worn smooth, 'nd polished by rain,
There she lies, waiting for com'ng dawn;

Time's folds, stir in dawns breeze,
That branch of past time 's leading me astray;
Morn'ng sky, blue, and calm,
Wondering, has youth already gone by?
The night-birds songs are now of passing grace
Early dawn dearer to me, than this shadowy verse,
Among the trees calm, sunlight rise,
On pools hidden by birch and those ancient pine's;

I drank from that sweet crystal pond,
Where shadows are hidden, as the day draws on,
Daylight graces now in the summer's dells,
I hurry on my journey, amidst the summer's day gay,
To find that incense bowl, so divine,
Then light twinkle it's last waning rays,
A scintillating shower of that golden light,
And beneath those skies is a woman, full of mysteries;

I 'll seek her dur'ng that spring day of flowers,
To save her of the dark waves, nature's bestows,
I will fondly bend o'er and seek rest,
My creations are alight within her sight;
Amidst butterflies and roses gay, I wonder,
Is it all a loving dream,
To mingle soul with soul, And for thy breast to rest.

HISTORY

That woman that reigned once those cold fens,
Forlorn, she was, unable to cheat too well,
Her castle, once uphill 's now buried in dark glens,
Over near that stream, still 'nd filled with the trouble it befell;

Where it once in tranced summers light,
The years expired after her descend and cold display,
Now on wings of gold, amber and pure white,
She replays her sulphureous dreams, for 's this day;

Evil has build castles in our soul bound to that cold night,
A place with panels, gilded with sombre opulence,
Only the setting Sun, colored her life, with rich a light,
Only time reigns, now that th' ancients have left, ignoring the
difference;

But darkn'ss recedes, mountains and dales 're brightening,
Sun's glimmer arrived, after that nocturnal sky,
Intermingling with the worlds whose shadows 're lightning,
Air is heavy still with vivid rumors, on the days gone by;

In summers time when that glowing dawn is lit,
I think of that reign, past now and far away,
Castles and dreams of late, all but quit,
All there is left, is the truth to be told of that ancient day;

We might pity our royal foe,
Accept the venomed dart of hate,
Those words and songs on that painted tableau,
And the touch of her enchanted flesh we did desecrate;

For we all desir'd color and order evermore,
A confusion of our vision,
A dream where hope weds indecision ever more,
Honor and intrigues we see, during that hour of contrition.

START OF SUMMER

I walked my soul's path,
>> With young greens shown all 'round,
Sky above, 's blue, but fill'd with scorching wrath,
>> Waiting I'm, hands clenched, for the battle-call to sound;

Is that angel of light, ready to fight,
>> Am I look'ng for that promised Sun in vain?
In that vast empty plain, 'twas once a place of delight,
>> Summer approaches, and winter w'll return to its chilly domain;

Deposed of its snowy throne, and 't has stopped it's frosty dance,
>> Now we can run through those field, soft and dewy,
With sweetness in the still colorless air, we advance,
>> Warmer now light 's ardent but bright 'nd pretty;

As the birds sing the verdure boughs gladly 'll bend,
>> In my solitude profound as natures gates fall,
That glorious freedom without the chill winter's send,
>> Now sitting in that ruddy light, it's days last call;

Shadows shoot across those still barren lands,
>> As the Sower scatters it's seeds, to and fro,
Gone is that young light, as darkness expands,
>> And the night passes my brow;

Alas, morning brings Summer's light from the sky's above,
>> Bells gently ring,
Birds sweetly sing of that future of love,
>> I face that confusion of vision that Spring brings;

Room's are wide and open to that young turquoise sky,
>> Sun still that golden pinhead, swelling as day grows,
The hour chimes, as my pen that writes these lines, I cannot deny,
>> I'll hide all my memories, now only morns rosy blush st'll shows.

AMOUR IN VAIN

Love, as roses are alluring, her rose-briars will hurt,
Wild roses blossom's in this early spring,
Its briars protecting her from her sure fall.

A delicate flower to send forth its profound scent,
In that sunny green vale, I lay,
Thinking of love, as birds caroled joyfully.

While there, I took her heart to me,
Wondering about all those bright things to be,
When winter's time is here, all will vanish.

Then my visions will be in vain,
But as earth echo's ends,
And winter's naked tomb is no longer there.

Love will cease like a night's dreams, floating away,
Leaving me with that rose scent, and my creation true.
And thinking of the briar's hurt.

UNKNOWN

I adore you, my frivolous one,
My terrible passion!
With the devotion as an artist,
My idol, my love.
In these deserts and great forests wild,
Your mind has unfamiliar attitudes;

It's a secret riddle,
On your body the perfume prowls,
And your charms are like the sun;
Your body, your breasts,
And your languid poses, delight me,
The sweetness and the kisses I so love,
I love you

AUTUMN SPIRITS

They tell me she's lovely,
That autumn, but I did not see nor hear of her infernal secrets,
As a lullaby whose hand a long sleep invited me,
When winter's snow will cover my body;

My empty spirit is gone now,
Once I had love but it was a tiring wrestling of the days,
That love in in my letter box gave me the fatal blow,
Goodbye, my Love.

DAYBREAK

Morn's pale sun unfolds,
Within that turquoise ceiling,
And all the desires it's beholds,
The sun's young and still unfeeling;

Yes, I dwell lone near those rugged peaks,
Amit's dells verdant and waves of stone I cower,
Clouds ahead show as fleeting streaks,
Early dew's shakes in a scintillating shower;

Alas, guileless I wander,
Seeking that place yonder,
In m' native lands of light and sun tender,
Ancient trees of which I grow ever fonder;

We're happy dur'ng a Summer's day,
'mids flowers and that just mown hay,
Streams tumble through meadows and rocks,
Entwined in those visions of love, I cannot unlock;

That broad day of quivering disorder the sun 'll play,
I hear the birds passing grace,
And bell's gently ring that mid-day,
I weep for that sole delight I found the place I can embrace.

FOTHERINHAY

That youthful body, filled with riotous grace,
Ris'ng from that damp fen, early in th' year,
Flowers wait obedient for day' approach,
Proud and erect waiting for suns golden ray'

'twas the time she reigned of those cold Scottish fens,
Forlorn, she was, unable to cheat too well,
That castle, once uphill 's now buried in th' glens,
Over near that still stream, fill'd with the trouble it befell;

While once in tranced summers nights, we dance,
A world of veiled stars mirror'd in streams of mystery,
Through luminous trees we see the fullness of moon's expanse,
But we have to wait, for the queen's destiny;

With wings of gold emerald and sable, beheaded she was,
In that once isolated valley, amidst thos' broken, withered branches,
Now that foul spell is broken, as we know 'f king's faux pas,
Unfolding now are his plenitudes and hidd'n chances;

Alas life's crowded solitude shows th' fragility of those affairs,
Summer has ended, flowers fade and whither, following queens dead,
Now autumn is here and gone ar' the ancient tyrants and their heirs,
Amidst those cold wild winter storm we see all the stories we'e misread.

*Fotheringhay Castle in, was a favoured residence of Richard of, who
became Duke of York and a powerful magnate. Married to Cecily
Neville of the House of Neville, an influential family in northern
England, he fathered two future kings: Edward IV and Richard III,
and the latter was born at Fotheringhay Castle in 1452.*

*Mary, Queen of Scots , spent her final days at Fotheringhay, where she
was tried and convicted of treason. Elizabeth I of England officially sign
her death warrant, She was beheaded on a scaffold in the castle's great
hall on 8 February 1587.*

THE LIE OF LOVE

The days sears like boiling liquid,
Yes, they simmer in the air where they linger, as predicted;

The land's oscillating, crunchy and dry,
The sunlight, like boiling water, cascades down from the sky;

Streams of light, sizzle and absorb me,
Burned crumpled leaf's flutter down 'n that hot air, I see;

Hiding the azure sky streaked with white lines rife,
Rushing forward, to absorb th't pleasure of life;

Yellow, golden and white streaks, grasping,
Those radiant beams of pleasure that 're passing;

I have seen you, yes, m' darling,
While I sing, but my song is in a slow pace but st'll sparkling;

A song filled with those hidden lies,
And promises I cannot fulfill or reply.

DAYDREAM OF CREATIONS

Dur'ng that morn's mist that's ripp'd and torn at its peaks,
I see the lark saluting sun's light of th' day,
Hoping already f'r the glories it seeks,
After the dark glitters the eternity's display;

While sun rise' newly and so bright,
Hiding my night's dreams and its darkness dim,
Vainly, birds try to outstrip the runs of racing light,
Like fire burning holding them in its fiery brim;

Now my trail of wavering footsteps is fading,
I am encircled by that throbbing, tyrannical light,
A luminosity, 'n a profound way, persuading,
As if my unborn fulfilments are waiting for tonight;

My future, fluttering as an injured sparrow,
My creations still not finished, hide in m' dreams,
Time's running untethered, swift as 'n arrow,
Solitary, is m' subterranean vision it seems;

In my abyss of dreams, I write and paint my destiny,
With passion I pour over my work,
Facing strangers with tenacity;
Hiding from the phalanx of admires and their hidd'n quirks;

I indulge in my creations,
And see the trees of my endless forests,
Beside that stream of Christal water and natur's innovations,
I watch the blood red sunset falling with birds chorused.

DREAMS AND FOG
HAVE FLOWN

On that summers evening down the path I go,
That last sun, the hearth and tenderness I beloved,
All of ignorance of the birds that fly thy for show,
I cannot distinguish day from night, as I am unloved;

Long journeys slow trains, rain and snow,
This morn clouds is edged with silver,
Clouds suddenly appear where that watery space grows,
As garments showing what they 'll deliver;

At age of us, thine eagle's goes on its soaring flight,
And sweeps beyond the view,
Where it cannot see the dark horizon in the skies still bright,
Or the wild storms of want and woe still new;

But in that glistering sunlight of God's new day,
When dream and fog have flown thither,
On that velvet sward, morns pearly dewdrops play,
As through all seasons fairies guard, the flowers until they
whither;

In that rose-scented time out west,
Something sweet is there to be blest,
Ss dream mingles with thy sister rose,
She would tell me, yes all my fears and woes.

THAT GREEN BANK

Through ancient forest, that brook flowed as a raving tides,
Rushing through that half-lit glade, raving tides
Past birches wet and shining bark sides,
That mystic fear that my senses is not betrayed;

Amidst that gloomy umbrage of my mind's eye,
I sit under those giant elms boughs deformed and unkept,
As my feet are intertwined with creepers twine gone awry,
I struggle with my inner life, only God knows what a human
'll accept;

Alas, I seek that love that will be it that thorns or rosse allayed,
As I sleep on that green bank of light and shade,
My mind, whose essay is free, fearless and wild,
No soft pensive dreamy muse are need to be beguiled;

How quickly came that darkness tonight,
From that sky naught of light,
O, Venus show me your starry spark,
And your youthful spirit wild,

I am free from emotions past
With my mint purely cast
And the poets blessing take this pure and holy love-light,
For once, I wis to use that unfettered verse I write;

High upon that summits craggy cliff
Reigns that sun deep, frowning at ocean's whiff.

THESE COLORED BOWERS

Those angels whisper to one another,
Amidst, those earnest woes or other,
My soul dreams of solace,
And gods bland response;

In sun and shadows, I have journeyed long,
Waiting for that kiss upon my brow, as a song,
So that my days will be a dream,
Is it a vision of me 'r none I can redeem;

The tide of time is flowing back to me as if born,
Dur'ng that sheeny summer's morn,
Those stately cedars, and rosaries with scented thorny themes,
While in that hollow vaulted dome that river stream'd in it seams;

Thought's rooted in the garden of my mind,
While thou camest in that morn's mist behind,
Thou comest not to shows those flaunting vines,
While I wait for that matin song waken'd and shines;

As the newness and boldness that my art does devours,
Amidst my dwelling and these colored bowers,
Looking at the set of the day,
And those maidens passing away;

I loved that doleful wind, still unshorn,
A melodious air, forlorn.

WALKS IN BEAUTY

As this world is too much with us,
Little we see of nature that we can discuss,
On this beauteous evening calm,
One I do respect as a balm;

With festivals of newly born liberty,
Oh, who can recite that rhyme in infinity,
Of when we fly higher towards,
I would, If I was a careless a freeborn soul, without rewards,

She walks in beauty as moonglow glints,
Under starry skies, cloudless without tints,
I meet her aspect of her eyes,
As heaven's daylight denies;

She is soft, calm and eloquent,
Smiles that win a heart magnificent,
Although caves are measureless to man's plazas,
She'll find those romantic chasms;

With towers and walls girded round as transplanted,
A savage place, waning and enchanted,
In visions I once saw, where moon makes its lonely alleys,
With beams reverend and strong rallies;

Candles I will give to you, flames fly as finches wings,
As I plot my art for that landscape left fallow when ploughed.

MORN'S DUST THOU PART

Many generations have trod, did trod and still trod,
That silver dusk is appearing unshod,
As vaulted shadows did shatter,
We hear the drum of morn's play and patter;

Morn is abed as daylight slumbers,
Claws lie still, not alive of what she encumbers,
As we listen to those strong syncopated tunes rife,
While days sleep is still loose from its dream of life;

Today drinke with me, and kiss the cup,
This day has over brimm'd their clammy cells,
As we sit careless on that granary floor,
Thy hair lifted by that winnowing wind ashore;

Crickets sing now with treble soft,
As sedge withers along lakes shore where winds waft,
And that is why I sojourn abroad,
Across that sea in spite 'f what they saw was flawed;

Morn's dust thou part, the grave is not your goal,
Art is long while time is fleeting without control,
In this world's field 'f battle,
Learn to labor and to wait without tattle.

Time's winged chariot is near,
Thought that iron gate of life we fear,
We stand still as no strength will appear.

RAINDROPS FALL

Oh, sweetness, how often did I dream,
Strange and unknown, of that sky so extreme,
Where the winds wept as a bassoon,
And I pass that place where flowers 'll grow soon ;

A place of heavy perfumes and warm poisons,
Drowning my senses and all reasons,
That last moon is still red on that misted horizon,
And the poplars serried and stretch to meet my coming sun;

That flight of birds is a dark complexity,
Trees tremble as the winds rocks them with intensity,
Morn's light renders all a mordant blue,
I hear those whispered words, deceptive but with charm;

That left our souls silent but inwards singing,
But the faint color, 'twixt the leaf's of aspen flows, is clinging,
A leaf-fringed legend still hounds my time,
While I try to improve that flowery tale of my rhyme;

Now, my heart leaps and stalls,
Seeing those brief raindrops fall,
As a legend of what a fallen race did befall.

WINDS WANDER

Behold that field, to be cut, filled with a singing sound,
A plaintive song a melancholic strain still profound,
It is a delight, being among the grains and rills,
Not sleeping among those wild hills;

Nights are chilly but not dark,
While clouds spread thin, high and stark,
It is that month before May,
When birds, thou wert not free to play,

Alas, all earth and air and nights so bare,
As I sing hymns unbidden with care,
That delight and sound,
Better than all measures I ever found;

As the winds wander along the shore,
A serene morning mingling, burning but ready to explore,
Time overshadowing life and the dead we knew,
As I weep in that morn's dew;

Now that incense hangs upon those trees,
While art pours forth of thy soul across those seas,
Was it a vision or a waking dreams,
A silent stream, a labyrinth, full of hidden pleasure it seems.

ELEGANCE AND ECSTACY

No flock can range this valley free,
As high up on those craggy rocks I see with glee,
The reigns of that sun with its gold'n lonely face,
Now amidst the rigors of time, without grace,
That ceaseless wind blows, icy as I retreat,
Trapped between the groaning forest and where that sea meets;

Beaten by multitude of boundless harmonies, we possesses,
In that wild time, as tenderly we try to hide our caresses,
While that music in my soul I bore,
It did not stop long after it was heard no more;
We played those long serenades,
In those singing glades;

We whirl with elegance and ecstasy,
And those joyous retorts I see in that grey sea,
Calm in that half-light with branches surround,
And that vague languor we found,
We lull in that sweet russet grass,
So I can convince you, stopping that impasse;

While evening falls and the nightingales sings,
We speak words, we scarily hear what that bird brings,
Green trees rear above our roof, in folded pleats,
As God reaps and gathers, framed where his nature meets.

I DESIRE THAT FOREST

During those leaf-strewn gales,
Oft I dream those penetrating tales,
Of you, those lines and consoling grace that shines,
Uttering those tones fines,
That wind 's harsh and unkind, filled with grief,
I live in that land of vines and th't perfumed light,
But I desire the forest and fens before me, despite;

My dreams of you, your charm and tender songs,
Your auburn hair is like a flame where love belongs,
Inspiration, splendid and dominant,
With those lightsome eyes so profound,
Tranquil in twilight dens we walk
Those dark designs, void of envy and talk;

Now before the light quite fails,
Your glance drowns that morn tale,
As I glance o'er that wood's brow,
Full of wandering airs and what we endow,
Misty and opulence in that moons light,
Soft rain plays that summers song of delight;

Although my heart and soul reflect that time as one,
I have fled that tender but fatal one that's in control.

RINGING RHYME

Wherefore should I lay my heart, bare to befall,
We know on every tree hangs trouble, ripening till its fall,
Give thou ear that gentle lay,
In that cool day of early May;
  Sleep, darksome and deep,
  Up there wide, in my sleep;

Tender and caring, visions of the end, when sleep holds,
Pensive we stroll after that dream enfolds,
We hear that singing of that lonely bird's song,
Warbling the praises of that absent one's still young;
  Thou comforts as music often does,
  In the sun gilded air with clement time's grace;

Aft'r this the ringing rhyme 'll glide, as it must,
It is holding inspiration in mistrust,
As we feel those leaf strewing gales
As wolves run down the mad inclines;
  I know misery knows no allay,
  And hear those feeble birdlings wail;

Hear, I'll drink this universe as it recurs,
Unblemished, she is as that rose that not often concurs,
But whose eyes sparkle like my spurs.

DAWN IS SMILING

In those deliriously loving hours,
And the neglect, as darkness lours,
Our lips are slack and eyes blurred,
Her voice a subtle musical tone occurred;

While that lark still climbs up that dawn sky,
That gilded note sounds in reply,
Hunting horns, from far away,
As my fond dreams carries on, in their fight to play;

In the radiance of my dreams,
Summer has seized me, it seems,
From that shaded nook I spy its summers light,
I wait for th't glory as Sun's red degrees ignite;

Amid the discord of skies state serene,
I glean that place where I find pearls unseen,
As dawn smiles and dew covers your white wings,
We seek those clouds of water, where lovers sings;

I flirt with that flower filled with intoxication and delight,
And fain I would paint thou art when I'm near at night.

IT VESPER 'S DONE

Behind those deep-leaved boughs,
The Reaper ploughs,
While I write words with hell-fire hidden and gleaming,
As the eagle soars far above that place of our dreaming;

That uneasy wind is rising as roses are dun, In
my abode, amidst the cornfield's run,
My hearth revives it vespers now done,
While I listened to her and her azure
lidded sleep, th's begun;

I see delicates so gathered with glowing hand,
Wreathed silver, sumptuous it does stand,
Awake, or in that silver shrine I will take my rest,
After days toil and many a quest;

Let not ambition foil their useful toil,
I rest with those flaunting flowers on garden's soil,
Up yonder a murmur rose,
From were once that garden smiled close;

I frowned at the seas foaming flood,
Am I that eagle, screaming and passes by for blood,
Fair laughs at morn's helm,
As Sun proudly rides it's azure realm.

DEAD IS DONE

From red to green, yellow is not there,
We moved quick, following th' stampede of the cattle 'n despair;

Rain, hay and wet wood smell was 'n the air,
But odd noises were heard, something rare;

In that unfenced country green 'nd soft,
That ground was soft and kind;

Melting underfoot and soft 's pulp,
As those riverbank's long soft rigs;

Oft I have glideth high,
To say farewell of m' youth as times might;

In those garlands of clouds I'll hang,
I see those lakes where moons light sprang;

Death has done all that dead can do,
Without offence and disgrace due;

In that hillside, by the folds, with Gods patience, and man's scorn,
Larks fly strong they are on the wing, in that world they were born;

I ponder of that past,
Laid out all of it at last;

While all those lost stars seek a reason to bloom,
Along the glimmering shades and sympathetic nightly gloom.

AUTUMN IS HERE

From behind where that soft Moon spreads,
In a dim eclipse, that twilight sheds;
I wrestle with that wind and ocean,
O ye, tumbling waves of that dark sea's motion;

Dur'ng that night, we slumber in Moon's pale light,
Were we share that fierce and far delight;
With thoughts deep, yet clear, gentle and not dull,
Without rage but strong and full;

As I am taught to make my muse sing,
Without pruning my created wing;
Now that winter is close,
Withered leaf's dance at our soiled feet most lost;

This autumn is now nearly a year old,
I hear those bellows of the stags seeking females to be controlled;
Fruit has now fallen on that cooling ground,
Playing with the wind shredded golden leaf's unbound;

Those leaf's, torn by autumn's wind without returns,
While stars look at those drunk'n birds;
Picking up that ripe harvest as dawn wears,
And wind and sea castrate that now barren oceans shore.